I0154863

Spotlighting the Gospel

SPOTLIGHTING THE GOSPEL

Clarifying the Gospel and its Biblical Response

Student Edition

John Thomas Clark, Thm, DMin
Tetelestai Press

Spotlighting the Gospel
© 2024 Copyright by John Thomas Clark
Published by Tetelestai Press

No part of this publication may be reproduced, stored
in a retrieval system, or transmitted in any form or by
any means, electronic, mechanical, photocopying,
recording, scanning, or otherwise, except as permitted
under Section 107 or 108 of the 1976 United States
Copyright Act, without the prior written permission of
the Publisher. Requests to the Publisher for
permissions should be sent to Tetelestai Press,
info@gracenewnan.org

ISBN: 978-1-7353359-7-1

TABLE OF CONTENTS

ACKNOWLEDGEMENTS

Spotlighting the Gospel was born out of a desire to provide a helpful tool for disciple-makers. Since the year 2000, I have had the privilege of being exposed to the clear, distinctive Biblical teaching regarding the gospel and the Biblical response to the gospel. Before that time, I was lost in a sea of confusion regarding the gospel and the Biblical means by which a person can be saved. In many ways, I did not know if I was *coming* or *going,* and I did not realize that much of what I believed regarding this issue was extremely contradictory and nonsensical. As a result, I lacked the assurance of my salvation, and, ultimately, I lacked a full appreciation for the *finished work* of Jesus Christ. These two things are the passion behind this project and this study! If on a scale of one to ten, your value for the finished work of Christ is an eight, I hope this study takes you to a nine. If it is at a ten, I hope it takes you to an eleven (if that is possible).

This concept of a fill-in-the-blank study comes from my exposure to this method through the mission organization Disciple Makers Multiplied (www.dm2usa.org), which is led by one of my mentors, Bret Nazworth. This method has been such a helpful tool in equipping disciple-makers all around the world.

The actual content of this booklet is a combination of my own teaching along with heavy reliance upon many other resources. I was first introduced to the concept of gospel clarity through the teaching ministry of Pastor Dennis Rokser at Duluth Bible Church in Duluth, Minnesota. In 2000, a dear friend of mine gave me a cassette tape of Pastor Rokser's teaching on gospel clarity, and the teaching changed my life! Additionally, Bret Nazworth, founder of DM2, included me on a trip with him to Sierra Leone to train pastors in 2012, and it was there that I assisted him in teaching Romans 1-8. In the appendix of the DM2 manual, there was a section entitled *What the Gospel Is, and What It Is Not*. As we taught that section, I had the privilege of watching lightbulbs go off in the minds and hearts of the pastors we were training. This, too, was life changing for me! I have also had the privilege of watching this take place in Liberia, West Africa, in work with pastors and church leaders there.

Hence, this project was birthed in my heart and mind. My desire was not to simply duplicate tools that were already in the marketplace or even to provide another book on gospel clarity (of which we do need more); but rather it was to provide a study tool that could enable someone to meet with others in a one-on-one or small group, interactive setting with booklets and fill-in-the-blank materials. I am praying this booklet will be used by God, according to His desire, to ground and establish new believers in the gospel message and put them on the road to future disciple-making endeavors of their own!

By His Grace,

John Clark, Thm, DMin

DEDICATION

First and foremost, I give God all the praise and glory for His faithfulness in exposing me to sound Biblical teaching regarding the gospel and its Biblical response. Each day, I rejoice more in the finished work of Jesus Christ, and I am thankful for the men who have clearly taught me the wonderful work of my Savior, which has been a life-changing, life-altering truth for me. It is hard to express in words how truly grateful I am!

I am thankful for my wife, Carrie, my best friend in life. Next to trusting Jesus Christ as my Savior, marrying Carrie was the best decision I have ever made. She has supported me in so many different ways throughout our marriage, and I cannot say enough words to express the honor and love that I have for her. Even with this book project, she functioned as my unofficial "grammar policewoman" in the writing process, and she provided her unending love, support, and encouragement! It is also awesome to walk through life with someone who is like-passioned and like-minded in the area of gospel clarity.

I am so thankful for our kids (Abby, Cody, Riley, Sadie, and Tobin), who are beautiful blessings to both Carrie and me. I am truly blessed as a father to have children who also support me in my teaching ministry. To have my children tell me that they *enjoy* my teaching and emphasis and that I am their favorite Bible teacher brings tears to my eyes. It is hard to explain in words how much I love these treasures. I pray that with each and every day of their lives, they see the value of what Jesus did for them!

I am grateful to my parents, Larry and Kathy, who raised me in a Christian home and shared the gospel with me at five-years-old. Sadly, my dad, who was truly one of my best friends, passed away in 2019 from Lewy Body Dementia. Today, my mom remains one my biggest supporters and claims me as her "favorite Bible teacher," which is crazy for her to say after all the grief I put her through in my teen years.

I also want to give a special thanks to my friend and co-laborer in the gospel, Josh Miller, who designed the cover of this book and also helped put the finishing touches on the entire project.

I also want to extend a special thanks to Emily Miller, my administrative assistant, who made this project a reality with her hard work in formatting the manuscript into book form.

I also want to extend a big thank you to the two men who helped film and edit all of the teaching videos for this book. Thank you to Bradley Mullinax and Robert Demurjian for the hours they dediated to this task!

In addition, I want thank the following men who agreed to read through and provide critique of the manuscript at different stages along the way: Robert Ambs and Rob Armstrong.

I also want to show appreciation for my current leadership board at Grace Community Fellowship in Newnan, Georgia. These men are huge supporters of any project or idea that further promotes a clear gospel message!

Last, but not least, I want to give a special thanks to the men who agreed to allow me to use their materials for this project! Each of these men's response when I visited with them about this project was exactly the same: "Use any of my material that you want! As long as it furthers the gospel, I am in!" Praise God for men like this! These men include: Bret Nazworth (www.dm2usa.org), Pastor Dennis Rokser (www.gracetruthbible.org), Pastor Tom Stegall (www.duluthbible.org), (www.gracegospelpress.org), and Pastor Michael Corcoris

IDEAS ON HOW TO USE THIS STUDY

1. Personal Study: Use the teacher edition for your own personal study to aid you in comprehending the gospel more clearly and to deepen your understanding of the Biblical gospel response, which is having faith, belief, or trust in the finished work of Christ alone.
2. One-on-One Study (with You Leading the Study): Maybe you know of someone who could use clarity in the area of the gospel and its Biblical response. If you are willing to lead the lessons yourself, here are some ideas and situations where it might be useful:
    a. For a believing friend who has never been exposed to the gospel distinctives.
    b. For a new believer who is hungry and growing spiritually.
    c. For your teenager or grown child over a weekly trip to the donut store, your favorite restaurant, coffee shop, etc.
    d. For anyone who might be willing to meet in a non-threatening, one-one-one situation.
3. One-On-One Study (with You Utilizing the Teaching Videos): Maybe you have someone in mind who you would like to do the study with, but you are not "up to" leading the study yourself. No problem! Utilize the FREE companion videos (found by utilizing the link from the QR code in the student book) and go through them with another person.
4. Small Group Studies: Maybe you can get a small group of people together who are willing to engage in different types of Biblical study. This could be one of the tools in your arsenal. You have two options, just like the one-on-one options mentioned above. They include:
    a. If you feel comfortable teaching/leading the study yourself, you could purchase the teacher edition for yourself and then get the student edition for everyone else.

b. If you do not want to teach the study yourself, you could utilize the FREE companion videos (found utilizing the link from the QR code in the student book) and go through them with your group.

5. Sunday School: Same instructions apply here as the ones for the small group studies that is listed above. It would be beneficial for each Sunday school participant to have their own student edition.

6. Homeschool Curriculum: For families looking to add some additional Bible studies to their child(ren)'s homeschool curriculum, this could help fill that need. It would be perfect to utilize the student edition and have the children watch the videos, fill in the blanks, and even do their own follow-up assignments to assess their understanding of the content.

Want to watch this book being taught?
Scan the code below!

LESSON ONE

The Gospel and its Biblical Response

I. **What the Gospel _____**

   A. **Defining the Word Gospel**

   1. The Greek word for _____is *EUANGELION.*

      a) The word *EUANGELION* can mean any type of good news. It is used seventy-seven _____ in the New Testament.

   2. The writers of the New Testament developed a _____ meaning for the word *EUANGELION*, or gospel, by articulating it (adding the word *the* in front of it).

      a) In Scripture, the word *gospel* came to mean _____ good news of salvation for all mankind.

      b) *EUANGELION* describes the saving message, the *Good News*, that an unbeliever _____ believe to be saved (1 Corinthians 15:1-4; Galatians 1:6-9).

   B. **Saved from What?**

   1. Implied in the term *salvation* and in Jesus' title as *Savior* is that mankind needs to be _____. The question becomes saved from "what?"

2. In other words, to truly appreciate *the* gospel, we must first recognize the bad news and the _____ for the *EUANGELION*.

    a) The bad news is simply this: as descendants of Adam, we are born _____ from God (due to Adam's first sin), and we prove, or demonstrate, our fallen position "in Adam" through personal acts of sin. (Psalm 51:5; Romans 5:12-14; 1 Corinthians 15:22).

    b) The Law of Moses was given to further _____this truth and to "shut our mouths" whenever we attempt to justify ourselves or declare ourselves righteous (Romans 3:19-20).

    c) The Law of Moses is unforgiving and permits no compromise. To keep the whole law, while offending in just _____ point, results in condemnation (James 2:10).

3. So what, though? Doesn't everyone sin? Yes, but sin has a _____, which the Bible describes as *death*.

    a) Death by definition is _____ (*See Appendix 1 – Types of Death*).

    b) The consequence of death is the result of our lack of perfect righteousness and our failure to obey   God's   Law.   God   must

_____ lawbreakers.

c) Death is described in Romans 6:23 as "wages
owed" or as something earned or

_____.

d) Additionally, this death penalty is a debt that
individuals can _____ pay
off on their own.

e) This *death* has multiple levels. First, it includes
_____ death, as every
human being dies physically. Second, it includes
_____ death, as every human
being is relationally separated from God at birth.
Third, it includes the "_____
Death," as every human being, who dies without
Christ, will be separated from God in the Lake
of Fire forever (Revelation 20:11-15).

4. Our two-fold problem (the problem in which we
need to be saved) can be summarized as: (1) We have
a debt we cannot _____, AND (2) We do
not have the _____ righteousness
needed to enter Heaven (God's perfect place).

C. The Gospel Described – It's Ability (Romans 1:16-17)

1. Romans 1:16-17 — The gospel is a powerful
message and the means by which God saves

_____ mankind. Notice that it is *Christ's* gospel, not a man-made gospel.

a) (vs. 16): *Power* (dunamis) – the word used here means able and capable, and it focuses on inherit _____. Thus, the gospel is able or capable to provide the salvation mankind needs.

b) However, notice there is a condition. The gospel is *only* able or capable to save those who _____ (more on this later).

c) (vs. 17): The gospel is what provides God's righteousness to undeserving sinners. Remember, we cannot do _____ to save ourselves!

2. The gospel is the _____ thing that takes care of our two-fold problem: (1) A debt we cannot pay, and (2) A perfect righteousness needed to enter Heaven.

3. The gospel is the objective, historical message of what God has _____ done to save us from His just wrath (our debt) and provide us with a righteousness that we could never obtain ourselves, thereby enabling us to live eternally with Him.

4. The gospel is not a subjective "how-to" method to move, push, or manipulate people through a salvation _____. It does *not* involve something you must do or continue to do in the future.

D. The Gospel Explained – The Irreducible Minimums (1 Corinthians 15:1-8)

1. The phrase *irreducible minimums* describes the bare minimum ingredients that you _____ have for a finished product. For instance, to have a peanut butter and jelly sandwich, your irreducible minimums are bread, peanut butter, and jelly. Without any of these, you do not have a peanut butter and jelly sandwich.

2. The gospel (*Euangelion*) has irreducible minimums as well. Those irreducible minimums of the gospel message can be summarized by _____ main "ingredients":

   a) The good news is about a _____ — the God-man, Jesus Christ.

   b) The good news is about a _____ — the actual, historical, and verifiable event of Jesus Christ's death and resurrection.

3. The Person – Two Components (Fully God and Fully Man)

   a) Christ is the Greek translation of the Hebrew word _____ (John 7:41).

   b) The Christ/Messiah was to be a _____ (Romans 1:3, 9:5).

   c) The Messiah is the Person (_____ of the woman) who has been promised to one day solve mankind's two-fold problem since the Garden of Eden where we are given the *first* glimpse of the gospel (Genesis 3:15).

d) The Christ was to be _____. Christ would be God residing with us (Isaiah 7:14; Romans 1:4).

e) Why is His Person important? Part of mankind's problem was the death penalty. The Christ had to be human to truly _____, and He had to be divine for His death to count for _____.

4. His Work – Two Components (Death and Resurrection)

    a) Christ _____ for our sins. Christ suffered spiritual, eternal, and physical death. He paid the *full* death penalty in all its multi-level aspects.

        1. _____ of His death

            a) According to the _____.… just as God said it would happen (Psalm 22:17-18; 69:11; Isaiah 53:3-6; Daniel 9:26; Zechariah 12:10; Luke 24:46).

            b) He was _____. You do not bury the living.

    b) Christ was raised on the _____ day.

        1. _____ of His resurrection

a) According to the _____ — just as God said it would happen (Psalm 16:8-11; Job 19:25-26; Isaiah 25:8; 53:10).

b) He was _____. The resurrected Christ was seen by many witnesses.

    i. _____ one of His closest friends and probably one of the most well-known Christians of all time (vs. 5a).

    ii. The _____ disciples who were still in doubt. Even though at that time, Judas was dead, and there were only eleven disciples, corporately they were still called the twelve (vs. 5b).

    iii. He appeared to over _____ at one event, most of whom were still alive at the time Paul wrote. If anyone wanted to interview these eyewitnesses in person, they could have (vs. 6).

    iv. James, Christ's _____-brother saw Him after the resurrection, and everyone knows that brothers know brothers. Someone who grew up with you can easily confirm who you are or identify you as a fraud (vs. 7a).

v.   The _____, the ones who He personally commissioned to share the facts of His death and resurrection with the rest of the world saw the resurrected Christ (vs. 7b).

vi. The apostle _____ saw the resurrected Christ. He had been a blasphemer and destroyer of the Church, but he saw the resurrected Christ and believed (vs. 8-10).

5. So, the irreducible minimums of the *Euangelion* are Christ's _____ (He is God, and He is man) and Christ's _____ (He died for our sins, and He rose again on the third day).

E. Man's Required Response – Faith

1. What response is _____ of man to be saved if the objective, historical, and verifiable work of Christ has already been accomplished?

2. According to the Scriptures, there is only one response required of man. It is _____ alone in Christ alone.

    a) There are _____ verses in the New Testament, which describe faith or belief in Christ as the only pre-requisite for salvation (*See Appendix 2 – "160 Verses"*).

    b) Acts 16:30-31; John 6:47; John 8:24; John 11:25-26; John 20:30-31

3. What is Biblical faith?

    a) The Greek words *pistis* (noun) and *pisteuo* (verb) literally mean believe in, _____ _____, trust in, or have faith in.

    b) *Believe* is a verb, and it requires a subject (someone who does the trusting) and an _____ (something or someone in whom to trust).

    c) The value of one's faith relies solely on the _____ or _____ of the object in which one trusts (Jeremiah 17:5-8).

    d) Faith is initiated by _____ the Word of God (John 5:24; Romans 10:13-17).

    e) Faith is excluded from the category of _____ by the Scriptures (Romans 4:4-5).

f) Since faith is not meritorious or some kind of work, it is _____ with the grace of God (Ephesians 2:8-9; Romans 11:6).

g) Since faith is not a _____, when you believe in Christ, it brings salvation to you as a _____, and then all the glory goes to God (Romans 4:20; Ephesians 2:8-9).

LESSON TWO

Gospel Response Clichés — (#1) Believe and Confess Your Sins and (#2) Give Your Heart (or life) to God

II. **What the Gospel is** _____

    A. Quick Review

1. Mankind's _____-fold problem is summarized as: (1) We have a _____ we cannot pay (death), AND (2) We do *not* have the _____ righteousness needed to enter Heaven (God's perfect place).

2. The gospel is the *only* thing that takes care of our _____-fold problem. The gospel is the *only* _____.

3. The gospel is the objective, historical message of what God has _____ done to save us from His just wrath (our debt) and provide us with a righteousness that we could never obtain ourselves, thereby enabling us to live eternally with Him.

4. So, what exactly did God do? He sent His Son Jesus Christ (fully God and fully man) to _____ for our sins and _____ again.

5. According to the Scriptures, there is only one response required of mankind. It is _____ alone in Christ alone. This is simply taking God at His Word and trusting in His _____ (Christ and His finished work) for our salvation.

B. What are the False Conditions for Salvation?

1. Many people in our day have an uncanny habit of syncretizing different responses to the gospel. This is an attempt to unite or harmonize pieces of information even if they are _____ or have different meanings.

2. This is why it is essential to critically _____ what the Bible says is the proper response to the gospel, knowing our own natural tendency to syncretize many false gospel response cliches.

3. It is actually when you begin to stipulate what the gospel is *NOT* or when you identify common Christian response cliches that many people often strongly _____! However, it is also when others begin to receive and enjoy more pronounced _____!

4. The apostle Paul had no problem stating _____ what the response to the gospel *IS,* and what it *IS NOT.* Turn to Ephesians 2:8-9 (See also Romans 4:5; Galatians 2:16).

   a) Regarding what it *IS*: Salvation is by _____, and it is through faith. It is also described as a gift!

   b) Regarding what it is *NOT*: Salvation is *NOT* of _____, and it is *NOT* of works. It is *NOT* for your glory, "so that no one can boast" (Ephesians 2:9).

    c) This brings _____ to mankind's required response to the gospel — knowing both what it *is,* and what it is *not!*

    d) Salvation cannot be both Christ's work and our own at the _____ time. It cannot be 99% Christ and 1% us. Unfortunately, many cliches used today require some sort of _____ to get saved.

    e) We either rely solely on the work of Christ or solely on _____; there is no middle ground (Isaiah 42:8; Acts 4:10-12; Romans 4:5).

5. Remember, the correct response to the gospel is *NOT* based upon an emotional response or feeling. It is based upon a response of faith to an objective message based on historical and verifiable _____.

6. The gospel is *NOT* something that goes on in our hearts, and it is not some experience that we have. It is something that happened to Jesus Christ _____ years ago.

C. Preparation for the Confusing Cliches

1. John 19:30 — When Jesus said, "It is finished (*Tetelestai*)," He meant that everything had been taken care of in terms of our _____-pronged problem. Our debt had been paid, and the righteousness equal

to God's righteousness was then able to be credited to our accounts.

2. In fact, the Greek word *Tetelestai* (translated as "It is Finished") has _____ meanings in Greek, and each has significance.

   a) "The debt has been _____." This one word has been found on paid invoices and receipts in the first century when one made his or her final payment.

   b) "The sacrificial _____ has been found." This one word was used by those groups searching for an acceptable, unblemished lamb in the fields for Passover sacrifices.

   c) "The job you gave me to do has been _____." This one word was used by servants to report back to their masters or authority figures to let them know that their task had been completed.

   d) Jesus Christ, in using this **one** word, literally said, "Dear Father, the debt has been paid, the sacrificial Lamb has been found, and the job You gave Me to do has been completed."

3. As we look at the clichés, take note of the following things:

   a) Are the gospel responses/cliches _____ for faith, trust, belief, or rely upon?

b) Do any of the gospel responses/cliches take care of the **penalty** for sin (death)? (*See Appendix 3 – Without the Shedding of Blood.*)

c) Do the gospel responses/cliches keep the _____ on Jesus Christ and His finished work for you, or do they put the spotlight on you, and something you must do to be saved?

d) Do the gospel responses/cliches add an _____ condition to the one Biblical condition of faith?

D. Gospel Response Cliche #1: Believe and Confess Your Sins

1. Now, *confession of sin* is a Biblical concept, but it is *not* a _____ for salvation. A person is *NOT* required to confess his or her sins to be saved.

2. Often, many people will lump the following phrases together: "Confess your sins," "Repent of your sins," and "Ask for forgiveness." People tend to do this because they think these phrases all communicate the ____ thing. However, as we will see, they do ___.

3. Some common misunderstandings of the phrase, *confess your sins*, are as follows:

a) First, many will teach you that you must remember and confess all your sins in order to get saved. However, it would be impossible to _____ every sin you had ever committed. Most of us cannot even remember what we had for dinner last night!

    1) Confession math: If you were to average three sins per _____ for your entire life, it would equate to 1,095 sins per year. If you were to live until you were eighty-years-old, it would mean that you would have to confess all 87,600 sins to ensure your salvation.

    2) Thus, your salvation would no longer be based upon your Sin-Bearer, who paid the penalty for all your sins, but rather it would be based upon your _____ and ability to recall and confess every sin you had ever committed.

  b) Second, due to this type of pressure on oneself to remember, one's understanding of the phrase would invite disconcerting introspection. A person who believed this would never be secure in his or her salvation for fear he or she had _____ some sin.

4. As discussed earlier, the Biblical response to the gospel is faith alone in the finished work of Christ alone. Thus, individuals will be condemned to the Lake of Fire, not because they failed to confess all

their sins, but because they did not

_____ in the Lord Jesus Christ, Who had

already paid for all their sins (John 3:18).

5. Consider some of the Biblical passages that use the word *confess,* and notice how they are often used to promote this misunderstanding (Romans 10:9-10; 1 John 1:9).

   a. Before we turn to those passages, let's first consider the meaning of the Greek word translated *confess.* The word is a compound word (**homologeo**), and it is derived from two root words — *homo,* meaning the _____ thing, and *logeo,* meaning to speak.

      1) Literally, the word *confess* means to say the same thing as or to _____ with.

      2) The word does not require _____ (crying or feeling remorseful) to be present. The word is *NOT* a _____ for the word *ask.* The word, in and of itself, has nothing to do with _____.

   b. Romans 10:9-10 is a passage that we will cover in more detail in a later gospel response cliché, but, for now, it is easy to see from the context that "sin" is *NOT* what is being confessed in this passage.

1) Clearly, what is being confessed in Romans 10:9 is "the _____," *NOT* sin. So, what does this mean?

2) The word *Lord* (**kurios**) has a generic meaning of lord, master, owner, or sir. It is generically a title of _____.

   a) But, based upon the word's use in the Septuagint (LXX) as well as Paul's intended audience (the Jews), Paul was most likely using this term as a more _____ term.

   b) The word *Lord* (**kurios**) is used synonymously with _____ in the Old Testament over 8,600 times in the LXX. One such occurrence is in Deuteronomy 6:4 in what is known as the *Shema*.

   c) This is significant because the Septuagint (LXX) was the Bible _____ that most Jews used in Paul's day. So, by using this word (*kurios*), Paul is making a strong statement of Jesus' deity (His true identity).

d) So, what does the phrase, *confess the Lord Jesus,* mean? The Jews of Paul's day were to agree with God (and Paul) that Jesus was indeed God and thus qualified to save them from their sins. They were to "confess that Jesus is Yahweh (God)" (i.e., say the _____ thing about Jesus that God says about Him – He is Yahweh).

c. 1 John 1:9

1) In this verse, we have the phrase *confess our sins,* but is this speaking of how one gets _____, or is it speaking of something else?

2) The _____ of the entire chapter of 1 John 1 reveals its primary audience is those who are already saved. Thus, as we will see, the issue is fellowship and *NOT* salvation.

a) Consider that John uses the word *fellowship* four times in 1 John chapter 1. Fellowship is a family term for those _____ in the family. Fellowship is _____ used to describe unbelievers in relation to God.

b) Additionally, John includes _____ with his readers by using the first-person plural pronouns "we" and "our." Thus, whatever is true of John is true of his readers.

c) Thus, this passage with this exhortation to "confess our sins" is for someone who is _____ a believer, not a pre-requisite for someone to become a believer.

d) Confession of sin is, therefore, for the believer in order to _____ fellowship with God, not for the unbeliever to _____ saved. Confession of sin is God's mechanism to restore relational intimacy with Him when a believer has sinned.

e) God does not want His children to _____ for forgiveness, but rather He wants them to tell Him exactly what they did _____. This is confession! And, when we confess our sins, He is faithful and just to forgive us our sins and restore us back to fellowship.

E. Gospel Response Cliché #2: Give Your Heart or Life to God

1. The saving message of the gospel does not involve _____ something to God in return for salvation.

2. If salvation is attained through an exchange of any type, it is no longer a free gift but becomes something earned or _____ for. Grace is either grace, or it is not! (See Romans 11:6.)

3. This cliché gets everything _____. Is the gospel about you giving your life, your heart, or anything else to God, *OR* is the gospel about Jesus Christ giving His life for you? (See Galatians 2:20; Ephesians 5:2.)

LESSON THREE

Gospel Response Clichés – (#3) Ask for Forgiveness and (#4)
Pray the Sinner's Prayer

A. Quick Review

1. Mankind's _____-fold problem is summarized as:
   (1) We have a _____ we cannot pay (death), AND
   (2) We do not have the _____righteousness
   needed to enter Heaven (God's perfect place).

2. The gospel is the only thing that takes care of our
   ___-fold problem. The gospel is the only _____.

3. The gospel is the objective, historical message of
   what God has _____ done to save us from
   His just wrath (our debt) and provide us with a
   righteousness that we could never obtain ourselves,
   thereby enabling us to live eternally with Him.

4. So, what exactly did God do? He sent His Son Jesus
   Christ (fully God and fully man) to _____ for our
   sins and _____ again.

5. According to the Scriptures, there is only *one*
   response required of man. It is _____ alone in
   Christ alone. This is simply taking God at His Word
   and trusting in His _____ (Christ and
   His finished work) for our salvation.

B. Gospel Response Cliche #3: Ask for Forgiveness

1. The bottom-line question that individuals must ask themselves when using this cliché is the following: "_____ does one receive forgiveness of sins?" Is it by ASKING God for it, OR is it simply a benefit one receives when one puts his or her faith in Jesus Christ? Which response is _____?

2. "Asking" and "believing" are NOT _____.

    a) *Asking* someone for something implies the answer is in _____. In other words, the answer could be "yes," or it could be "no."

    b) *Asking* someone for something implies that the work or action still needs to be _____. Some generic everyday life examples include:

        1) "Dad, can I have the keys to the car?" (asking) – "Yes, here they are" (executed work).

        2) "Dad, can I borrow some money?" (asking) – "No, you cannot" (non-executed work).

        3) "Friend, can I stay the night at your place tomorrow?" (asking) – "Sure, here is the key to my front door" (executed work).

        4) "Will you help me change my flat tire?" (asking) – "I would love to, but I am already late for work" (non-executed work).

    c) In contrast to *asking*, Biblical faith implies that a work has _____ been done, and you are trusting in it to save you.

    d) Belief or faith trusts in a _____ outcome, whereas asking someone for something implies an _____ outcome.

    e) Because *asking* God for forgiveness, by definition, has a level of doubt implied, this often-used cliché is really a subtle form of _____ and is *NOT* faith.

3. You receive _____-*time*, *positional* forgiveness of sins, as an unbeliever, when you believe on the Lord Jesus Christ (Acts 10:43; 13:38-39).

4. And, as discussed in gospel response cliché #1, you receive *continual, fellowship* forgiveness of sins as a Christian when you _____ your sins (1 John 1:9).

    a) *Confession* means to say the _____ thing, and we are to say the same thing about our sin that God does.

    b) This is agreeing with God, or *naming our sin*, not _____ for forgiveness or just saying "sorry."

5. God had already determined how, when, where, and by what means He would provide the free gift of salvation, which _____ the forgiveness of

sins. He did so through the _____ of the Lord Jesus Christ on the cross of Calvary and Jesus' subsequent resurrection from the dead.

6. You will not find _____ in the Bible where unbelievers or believers are taught to ask for forgiveness of their sins! But, some may ask, "What about the Lord's prayer in Luke 11:4?"

    a) Luke 11:4 is part of the Lord's Prayer, as recorded by Luke, where he specifically states, "And forgive us our sins, for we also forgive everyone who is indebted to us...."

    b) How do we know that Luke is *NOT* teaching unbelievers how to get saved? Let's consider the context.

        1) The prayer starts with the words, *Our Father*, indicating those who are _____ a part of the family of God. This is *NOT* a prayer for salvation by an unbeliever, but rather a prayer of someone already in the family of God.

        2) The prayer is very much looking forward to the establishment of the Kingdom of God on earth through the long-awaited Messiah. Thus, the focus is on a very specific _____ in Biblical history (still future at this point).

3) The word *forgive* means "to send forth or away, to let go from oneself, or to dismiss from oneself." This is _____ to understanding WHY Jesus encouraged His disciples to ask for forgiveness here.

   a) In the Old Testament, sin was only *atoned for* or _____. Sin was never *taken away* or _____. This is why the word *forgive* (**salah**) is mostly used in the future tense in the Old Testament.

   b) This is also why what John the Baptist says in John 1:29 is such an incredible statement! He says, "Behold! The Lamb of God who _____ _____ the sin of the world!"

   c) The Old Testament saints were awaiting the day that the Messiah would take away their sins, as promised in their _____ Covenant (Jeremiah 31:31-34 – *verse 34*).

   d) Thus, in this prayer in Luke 11, asking God to forgive their sins was akin to asking God to *establish His kingdom and the _____ of the New Covenant.*

C. Gospel Response Cliche #4: Pray the Sinner's Prayer

1. Would it surprise you to know that there is no "sinner's prayer" found in the _____? Also, would it surprise you to know that there is never an _____ in the Bible of even one person leading another person in a prayer in order to be saved?

2. Please take a minute and flip to **Appendix 4: Different Versions of the Sinner's Prayer** and read it. You will notice that none of the versions of the prayer are the _____. If a certain prayer saved you, wouldn't you want to know if you were saying the right one or including the right things in your prayer?

3. The proper Biblical response to the gospel does not involve _____ a prayer or walking the aisle at church. Again, the Biblical response does *NOT* require you to DO something in the present but rather trust in something that _____ happened in the past.

   a) If praying a prayer were a _____ for salvation, the Lord would have made it abundantly clear and included this response in multiple passages of Scripture.

   b) If praying a prayer were a requirement for salvation, one would expect to see it born out for us in the _____ accounts in the Gospels, or the book of Acts, or clearly taught or instructed in the epistles.

4. Consider two passages that are often brought up to promote the response of praying for one's salvation. They include:

   a. Luke 18:9-14

      1) The key to _____ this passage, contextually, is verse 9. "Also He [Jesus] spoke to some who trusted in themselves [Pharisees] that they were righteous and despised others."

         a) Typically, parables have _____ major truth or principle that they are trying to communicate. In this parable, Jesus tells us exactly what that truth is in verse 9.

         b) Jesus is speaking to the self-righteous Pharisees, who thought they were better than everyone else because they were trusting in their own _____ keeping of the Law for their righteousness.

         c) Notice how the Pharisee (vs. 11) "stood and prayed thus *with himself.*" Everything he was doing was for show and to be noticed. He was exalting his _____ external righteousness.

d) To read an _____ principle or truth into this parable is to overreach in our interpretation of it. In other words, to make this parable a teaching on how one gets _____ by saying a prayer is to do damage to the original intent of the teaching.

2) The tax collector, in contrast, was not _____ upon himself for his righteous standing before God. He had a clear understanding of his own unworthiness.

a) Thus, his prayer was not one for salvation, but rather he was _____ his faith in God for his righteous standing and was doing so through prayer.

b) The prayer did *not* _____ him. He prayed because he was _____ *saved* (justified or declared righteous by God). The prayer just manifested his already present faith.

    b. Romans 10:13 – We will get into the full detail of the context of this passage in a later gospel response cliché, but, for now, consider the following observations:

        1) Notice that Romans 10:13 gives *calling on the name of the Lord* as a _____ to being saved. The key question when anyone sees the word *saved* in the Bible is to ask, "Saved from what?" What kind of salvation is in the mind of Paul here?

            a) Based upon his use and distinction of *obtaining righteousness and salvation,* seen earlier in the chapter, and based upon the fact that Romans 10:13 is really a quotation of Joel 2:32, it seems as if the salvation that Paul is referring to is salvation from the future great _____ period, leading into the Millennial Kingdom.

            b) The context of Joel 2 is the *Day of the Lord,* comprised of _____ the Tribulation (70th Week of Daniel) and the Millennial Kingdom.

        2) Notice the word order in verses 14-15. You have to work backwards to see the

_____ order. A

messenger is **sent**, that messenger **preaches**, the audience of the messenger **hears** the message, the audience **believes** the message, and then the audience **calls upon** the Lord.

a) So, by the time someone *calls upon the Lord,* he or she is already saved because he or she has _____ in Him.

b) For someone to say that these individuals are not _____ until they call on the name of the Lord would mean that they are not saved when they believed. If that is the case, they must explain why 160 verses in the New Testament teach faith as the only prerequisite for salvation (*See Appendix 2: 160 Verses Proving Justification by Faith Alone*).

5. Some may ask, "If I said a prayer to get saved, does that mean I am not saved?" If these individuals placed their faith in Christ and His finished work, then they were saved at that _____. Some who pray *the sinner's prayer* were probably saved a few moments

before they actually repeated the prayer, when they actually first trusted in Christ.

LESSON FOUR

Gospel Response Clichés – (#5) You Must Make a Public Profession of Your Faith

A. Quick Review

1. Mankind's _____-fold problem is summarized as: (1) We have a _____ we cannot pay (death), AND (2) We do not have the _____ righteousness needed to enter Heaven (God's perfect place).

2. The gospel is the only thing that takes care of our ____-fold problem. The gospel is the only _____.

3. The gospel is the objective, historical message of what God has _____ done to save us from His just wrath (our debt) and provide us with a righteousness that we could never obtain ourselves, thereby enabling us to live eternally with Him.

4. So, what exactly did God do? He sent His Son Jesus Christ (fully God and fully man) to _____ for our sins and _____ again.

5. According to the Scriptures, there is only one response required of man. It is _____ alone in Christ alone. This is simply taking God at His Word and trusting in His _____ (Christ and His finished work) for our salvation.

B. Gospel Response Cliché #5: You Must Make a Public Profession of Faith

1. This error implies that in order for one to be saved, one has to make a _____, public profession of his or her faith in Christ.

    a) Now, is it _____ to teach people who have believed to make public professions of their faith in Jesus Christ? No, this is exactly what we want those who are saved by faith to do in life through evangelism and even through water baptism, etc.

    b) However, if public profession were a prerequisite to be saved, then Christ's work on the cross to pay for sin was *NOT* _____. Individuals would have to add their **work** of *public confession* to Christ's work of dying for their sins in order to _____ their salvation.

2. Additionally, where would this leave people who could not speak (those who are _____), and where would this leave people who heard the gospel, and who put their faith in Christ, but then died before they were able to _____ confess Christ to someone?

3. Again, the reason this gospel cliché is even used is because the concept of public profession of Christ is _____! It is just *not* a prerequisite to be saved.

a) It is true that public confession will be rewarded in eternity, and denial will exclude one from reward, but it in no way _____ a person salvation.

b) If denial or lack of public profession is required for salvation, then the Apostle Peter could not have been _____ (ex. three crows of the rooster).

4. For some people, it seems they need a visible, measurable event to point to for them to feel that their salvation experience is _____. However, God sees faith! He does not need any behavior or prayer to make it *official* to Him. It is official the _____when a person trusts in the finished work of Christ.

5. Let's consider one of the more popular passages used to teach that one must make a verbal public profession of Christ as a requirement for salvation.

a. Romans 10:9-10

1) Verse 8 is the _____ in Paul's exhortation to the Jews (in verses 9-10) to believe on the Lord Jesus Christ and to stop pursuing their own uninformed way of law-based righteousness (See verses 1-4).

2) Paul is *NOT* giving a detailed _____ by which someone gets saved, but rather he is building off an Old Testament cross reference to teach faith-righteousness.

3) The Old Testament reference that Paul quotes is Deuteronomy 30:12-14, but as we will see, he makes some key _____ under the inspiration of the Holy Spirit.

   a) Paul mentions two key elements of his message, which are the two main _____ for his present-day Jewish brethren. Those obstacles are Jesus' identity and Jesus' resurrection.

   b) To communicate to his present-day Jewish brethren that this message of *faith-righteousness* was ____ to them and _____ to them, Paul uses the Deuteronomy passage to communicate this *nearness* since Moses used this concept regarding the Law.

   c) This is why Paul continues to use the words *heart* and *mouth* in verses 9-10. He is working off of Deuteronomy 30 and tying it with minor _____ and New Testament applications.

d) Whereas Deuteronomy 30 was focused on the Law, and what one must _____, Paul is focused on the Person/work of Christ, and what one must _____.

4) Let's consider the two obstacles in verse 9 for Paul's present-day Jewish readers:

a) ***Obstacle #1: Jesus' Identity — Confess Jesus as Lord:*** The Greek word translated *confess* (**homologeo**) means to say the _____ thing or to agree with.

   i. Notice, this is not a confession of _____ or a feeling sorry for sin. What then does *confession* mean in this context?

   ii. The Greek word translated *Lord* (**kurios**) has a generic meaning of lord, master, owner or sir. It is generically a _____ of respect.

   iii. However, it came to have a more technical use, especially as it related to the Greek translation of the Old Testament (the Septuagint or LXX). This word (**kurios**) is used of the covenant-keeping God of Israel

(_____ or Jehovah) over 8,600
times!

    iv.   So, these unbelieving Jews were to
confess that Jesus is _____ or Deity.
They were to _____ with
Paul and the Word of God that Jesus
was Yahweh (See John 8:24).

    v.   No Jews would confess this unless
they believed it were _____! Why
would they *confess* the Lord Jesus if
they had not first _____
that He was the Lord Jesus? (Verse
10 gives us this order: believe THEN
confess.)

    vi.   Confession is the _____ of denial.
If one denies that Christ is God, why
would that person trust Him for his
or her salvation?

b) ***Obstacle #2: Jesus' Resurrection –
Believe that Jesus Rose from the Dead***

    i.   To believe in one's *heart* is
synonymous with one's *mind* or the
center of one's being. Nowhere in
the Bible do the writers of Scripture
_____ between *head*
faith and *heart* faith.

     ii. The fact that Jesus is Lord (God/Deity) became clear when He _____ from the dead. Since God is described as the "Actor" in Jesus' resurrection, it means that God _____ Jesus' payment on the cross as sufficient.

   c) So, if Paul's readers believed either of these two things, then the other one, like a _____, would fall. If Jesus were Yahweh, then, of course, He could be resurrected, and if He was resurrected, never to die again, then He was Yahweh.

5. Verse 10 gives us the proper _____ between *believing* and *confessing*. It is *believe THEN verbal confession*. If verbal confession comes, it _____ belief.

6. Now, it must be pointed out that Paul uses two words here that are _____. They are the words *righteousness* and *salvation/saved*.

   a) When Paul uses the word *righteousness*, he is speaking of salvation from sin's _____. In the Western world, we would typically use the word *salvation* or *saved* to describe this.

    i.   Paul has been consistent with his messaging in the book of Romans concerning how one _____ the righteousness of God. It is by faith alone in the Person and finished work of Christ alone (Romans 1:16-17; 3:10; 3:21-26, etc.)

    ii.   When individuals _____ in Jesus, they immediately obtain the righteousness of God without delay. This obtaining of righteousness is called *justification* (See Romans 5:1).

b) When Paul uses *salvation/saved,* because of the eschatological (end times) context, he is referring to the *salvation of Jews* OUT OF the coming _____ period and INTO the coming Millennial Kingdom.

    i.   For the Jew, the Kingdom is _____ with the eternal state. The Western world/the Church speaks of *Heaven.* For Jews, they speak of the Kingdom.

    ii.   This is why Paul goes on to quote Joel 2:32 in Romans 10:13. The context of Joel 2:32 is the Day of the Lord (Joel 2:31), which is comprised of both the seven-year

_____ period AND the Millennial Kingdom reign of Jesus Christ.

iii. So, in Romans 10, Paul seems to use *confession* and *calling* interchangeably, or, at least, they are closely related if distinct. Both these actions are _____ by faith in Jesus Christ!

iv. Putting it all together, for Jews to be saved from the penalty of their sin and obtain the righteousness of God, they must put their _____ in the finished work of Christ.

v. When a Jew (or Gentile, for that matter) has done this, he or she is _____ _____ and will enter the Kingdom of God (See John 3:3ff).

vi. However, for the specific _____ of Jews living during the Tribulation period, they will be delivered (saved) from the Tribulation period when they *call on the name of the Lord Jesus*, but they will only do so if they have _____ believed in Him.

b. For a detailed look at another passage, see the "Extra Study" section for Lesson 4, where 2 Timothy 2:11-13 is also analyzed.

LESSON FIVE

Gospel Response Clichés – (#6) Ask Jesus into Your Heart

A. Quick Review

1. Mankind's _____-fold problem is summarized as:
   (1) We have a _____ we cannot pay (death), AND
   (2) We do not have the _____ righteousness
   needed to enter Heaven (God's perfect place).

2. The gospel is the only thing that takes care of our
   ____-fold problem. The gospel is the only _____.

3. The gospel is the objective, historical message of
   what God has _____ done to save us from
   His just wrath (our debt) and provide us with a
   righteousness that we could never obtain ourselves,
   thereby enabling us to live eternally with Him.

4. So, what exactly did God do? He sent His Son Jesus
   Christ (fully God and fully man) to _____ for our
   sins and _____ again.

5. According to the Scriptures, there is only one
   response required of man. It is _____ alone in
   Christ alone. This is simply taking God at His Word
   and trusting in His _____ (Christ and
   His finished work) for our salvation.

B. Gospel Response Cliche #6: Asking Jesus into Your Heart

1. This is probably the most common and most
    _____ of all gospel response clichés in
    modern day Christianity.

    a) One pastor estimated he had asked Jesus into his
        heart _____ times by the time he was
        eighteen years old! He claims to hold the
        unofficial *Guinness Book of World Record* for doing
        so.

2. The following are five Biblical reasons to _____
    ask Jesus into your heart.

    a. **_REASON #1_**: "Asking Jesus into your heart" is
        _____ found in the Bible.

        1) Nowhere in the Bible is anyone
            instructed to ask Christ into his or her
            heart to be _____, and nowhere in
            the Bible is there one example of this
            happening! (Past this, do we really even
            need another reason?)

        2) It is safe to assume that if you never
            listened to Christian radio, attended an
            evangelistic crusade, or went to a church,
            and all you did was _____ your Bible,
            then you would *not* conclude that you
            must ask Jesus into your heart to be
            saved.

b. ***REASON #2***: "Asking Jesus into your heart" is not how one is _____.

1) Acts 16:30-31, Ephesians 2:8-9, and many other passages teach us that we are saved by grace through _____ in the person and work of Jesus Christ.

   a) *Asking* someone for something implies that the answer is in _____, meaning it could be "yes," or it could be "no."

   b) Biblical *faith* implies that a work has _____ been done, and you are trusting in it to save you.

   c) Belief or faith trusts in a _____ outcome, whereas asking someone for something implies an _____ outcome.

   d) Because *asking* God for forgiveness, by definition, has a level of doubt implied, this often-used cliché is really a subtle form of _____ and NOT faith.

   e) Christ does not come into believers' hearts because they

_____ Him to; rather, it is a

direct _____ of believing

in Him.

c. ***REASON #3:*** "Asking Jesus into your heart"

requires no _____ of

the gospel to do it.

1) Remember the gospel is that Jesus Christ
(the God-man) died for our sins and rose
again. You can ask Jesus into your heart
without believing or even
_____ this truth.

2) Over the years, in hundreds of
conversations with people about
salvation, it is amazing to note that many
who have *asked Jesus into their hearts* do not
even mention _____ or His work!

a) In fact, many of these people go on
to describe how good works are
_____ to get saved or to
stay saved.

b) This is because their confidence has
been _____. Their confidence
has been directed to an event or a
process where they were told to ask
Jesus into their hearts (usually
through a type of *sinner's prayer*), and

thus their confidence is NOT in the

_____ work of Christ alone.

3) If someone were to ask you, "Do you know for sure you are saved and going to Heaven? If so, why?", the focus of your answer should be on the _____ _____ of Jesus Christ dying for your sins and rising again, *NOT* on some event where you asked Jesus into your heart. This is the _____ *event!*

d. **_REASON #4_**: "Asking Jesus into your heart" results in no _____ of salvation or brings a _____ assurance to people.

1) No one has ever been _____ by *asking Jesus into his or her heart!* In fact, no one can get saved by *asking Jesus into his or her heart!*

a) This is probably why many people who have *asked Jesus into their hearts* have done so more than _____.

b) Inevitably, this is because this response puts individuals' _____ upon themselves, *NOT* on Jesus Christ.

c) Unfortunately, for many of us, the _____ of our faith (what we are relying upon to save us) becomes the event where we *asked Jesus into our hearts,*

NOT the _____ of the finished work of Jesus Christ.

d) "Asking Jesus into our hearts" is an _____ object of faith, and deep down we know it, and it is why many of us have done it repeatedly.

2) Now, some people may have put their trust in Christ alone, but they are confused. However, they are truly saved because they put their trust in Christ _____, *NOT* because they *asked Jesus into their hearts.*

3) Because of the _____ that this false response creates, some typical questions and concerns that come up after one has *asked Jesus into their hearts* include:

a) Did Jesus Christ really _____ _____ when I asked?

b) Was I _____ enough when I prayed?

c) Did I say the _____ words?

d) How do I _____ He came in for sure?

4) This lack of assurance happens with *asking Jesus into our hearts* because we are shifting the issue of salvation to what we are

_____ instead of putting our trust in Jesus Christ, and what He has _____ done for us!

e. **_REASON #5_**: Revelation 3:20 does *NOT* _____ someone *to ask Jesus into one's heart*.

1) Interestingly enough, the words *ask*, *Jesus*, and *heart* are not even _____ in this verse, yet this is the common proof text to show that this false gospel response is Biblical.

2) As with every passage in the Bible, context is key. So, who is the original audience that John is writing to here? The _____ at Laodicea is the original audience of Revelation 3:20 (Revelation 3:14-22 is the full message to the Laodicean church).

3) Jesus is not describing how an _____ gets saved here, nor is He giving a call to unbelievers to respond to the gospel.

a) What is clear from the passage is that Jesus is _____ and _____ an overconfident, carnal local church.

b) This is a church who has mis-evaluated her own actions and determined that she is the epitome of _____ (vs.

17a). Jesus' evaluation was completely

_____ (vs. 17b-19).

4) In verse 20, what door is Jesus knocking on?
From the context, it is clear that He is
knocking on the door of the
_____, *NOT* the unbeliever's
heart.

   a) Jesus says that He will come "in to" him
   (into the _____ and over to that
   individual), *NOT* "into" him (to come
   _____ the individual's heart).

   b) This verse is about
   _____ with the
   Lord, as evidenced by the description of
   "dining with Him," for the believer,
   NOT salvation for the unbeliever.

**(See Additional Resources and 'Seven Reasons Not to Ask
Jesus Into Your Heart')**

LESSON SIX

Gospel Response Clichés – (#7) Repent "From" OR Repent "Of"
Your Sins

A. Quick Review

1. Mankind's _____-fold problem is summarized as:
   (1) We have a _____ we cannot pay (death), AND
   (2) We do not have the _____ righteousness
   needed to enter Heaven (God's perfect place).

2. The gospel is the only thing that takes care of our
   ____-fold problem. The gospel is the only _____.

3. The gospel is the objective, historical message of
   what God has _____ done to save us
   from His just wrath (our debt) and provide us with a
   righteousness that we could never obtain ourselves,
   thereby enabling us to live eternally with Him.

4. So, what exactly did God do? He sent His Son Jesus
   Christ (fully God and fully man) to _____ for our sins
   and _____ again.

5. According to the Scriptures, there is only one
   response required of mankind. It is _____ alone
   in Christ alone. This is simply taking God at His
   Word and trusting in His _____ (Christ and
   His finished work) for our salvation.

B. Gospel Response Cliche #7: Repent "From" <u>OR</u> Repent "Of" Your Sins

1. It may surprise you to learn that the phrase *repent _____ your sins* or *repent _____ your sins* is not found anywhere in the Bible.

2. The Word of God does not _____ repentance from sins in order to be saved, but every person who has ever believed upon Jesus Christ has repented of something.

3. So, what does it mean to *repent?*

   a) *Metanoeo* (verb) or *metanoia* (noun) are compound words in the Greek made up of two words — *meta*, meaning a _____ of place or condition, and *noeo*, meaning to exercise the _____, to think, or to comprehend.

   b) Putting these two together, the word means to change the _____, to relent, an after-thought, or a thought different from the former thought.

   c) Some _____, yet common definitions for the word *repent* are the following: feeling sorry for your sin, turning 180 degrees, and turning from sin and turning to God.

   d) It should be the desire of every Bible student to understand what Biblical words meant at the time in which they were written. This is the

_____ audience principle. What would the word have meant to the audience to which it was written during that specific time? This is part of the _____ of Scripture.

e) For a secular example of this, if you and I were to read something that said George Washington was _____, we would never read back into the text that he was a _____. We would understand that the normal, common use of the word *gay* in George Washington's day was to describe someone who was happy.

4. Let's consider a brief history of the use of the word *repent* in Greek:

a. ***Classical Usage (900-300 BC)***

1) The meaning of *repent* for both Plato and Xenophon (430-350 BC) was *changing one's* _____, and the meaning for Thucydides (471-400 BC) was *afterthought*.

2) Thucydides writes of a revolt in the City of Meytilene that the Athenian council had to address. On first judgment, the council decided to _____ everybody in the city, not just the ones who were revolting. However, the next morning they were said to

have *repented*, and they decided to kill just the
_____ in the revolt.

b. ***Koine Usage (300 BC-100AD)***

1) Polibius (208-126BC), in describing the Dardani people's plan to attack Macedonia while Phillip was away, used the word *repentance* to describe the Dardanis' change of _____ when Phillip quickly returned before they could strike.

2) Plutarch (ca 46BC-ca120AD) tells a story of Cypselus, who as a baby was supposed to be slaughtered by a few men sent to kill him. As they came to Cypselus, he smiled at them, and the men changed their _____ and decided not to kill him. Then, after they had left and had time to think about it some more, they changed their minds _____ and decided to find him again, so they could kill him, but they were not able to find him the second time.

c. ***Septuagint (LXX) Usage (250 BC) – Greek Old Testament***

1) There are _____ occurrences of the Greek words *metanoeo* (repent) and *metanoia* (repentance) in the Septuagint (LXX).

a) Thirteen pertain to _____ repenting or not repenting.

b) Four occur in the book of _____ and involve people thinking or changing their minds about something.

c) Three others involve sinners' changing their _____ about the nature of God or their sin.

5. What people change their minds about is not in or implied by the word *repent* itself. *Repent* can be used of _____, or it can be used of something _____.

6. Every verse in the Bible that uses the word *repent* tells you _____ specifically needs to change their minds or thinking, and _____ they need to change their minds or thinking about.

a) The moment that you believed in Christ, you changed your mind about what you used to _____ in and decided to believe exclusively in Jesus Christ. This was the message of John the Baptist (See Acts 19:4).

b) Repentance implies that no person is a _____ slate before salvation. Every individual is trusting in something or someone!

7. So, what went _____ with the meaning of the word *repent*, and why is its meaning so jumbled and confused today?

    a) Early in Church _____ (within the first couple of hundreds of years after the apostles), some false teaching arose regarding sin and God's solution for it.

    b) The false teaching went something like this: Original sin and all sins committed _____ _____ baptism were removed by baptism.

        1) Because of this belief, people waited until they were near _____ to be baptized.

        2) This kind of misunderstanding concerned pastors and Bible teachers of the day. Instead of directing them back to the Bible and the accomplishment of the finished work of Christ, they _____ to this teaching – the pendulum swung in a different direction.

    c) Their reaction to this false teaching went something like this: Repentance is the solution for _____-baptismal sins. However, repentance, as defined by these well-meaning theologians, involved _____ sorry for and _____ post-baptismal sins, as well as doing acts of _____.

d) To reflect this theology, the Greek words for *repent* and *repentance* were translated into _____ by words meaning, "do acts of penance" and "acts of penance."

e) So, when Jerome (ca. 340-420 AD) produced the *Latin Vulgate* translation of the Bible, he _____ the practice of translating *metanoeo/metanoia* (*repent* and *repentance*) with a Latin word meaning, "do acts of penance."

1) This Latin word *poenitentia* means *to make sorry, to grieve or displease, or doing* _____.

2) Because the Latin translation of the Bible (known as the *Vulgate*) became the _____ translation for many centuries (for 1,100 years), it caused a shift in the meaning of *repent* from *change of mind* to *sorrow for sin,* which has stuck for the most part in our day.

3) In addition to that, John Wycliffe (ca. 1320-1384 AD), while translating the first English Bible, _____ more heavily on the *Latin Vulgate* than he did on the original Hebrew and Greek texts.

4) The *Roman Catholic Douay* version (1609-1610) did the _____, and hence the reason for the _____ of the incorrect emphasis with the word.

8. For many people, when they say that one must repent *of* or *from* their sin in order to be saved, they mean that one must _____ *from sin.*

    a. They do not mean that the person must be perfect (sinless), but that they must have a desire to sin less *AND*, at some point, they should be sinning _____ they were before they were saved.

        1) How this is measured Biblically is a _____!

        2) Typically, the argument is made that if individuals are still continually or _____ committing the same sin as before they were saved, then they never really repented of that sin.

        3) If that is the case, however, how many times can individuals commit a sin after they get saved before the sin is considered "_____"? Is it once a year, once a month, once a week, etc.?

            a) And, if this is the case, what _____ passage can we go to for this clear delineation of teaching? The truth is that one does not exist!

b) If one were to use the incorrect definition of "repentance" promoted by so many people, wouldn't the logical conclusion be: "If you have truly repented (turned from sin), then you should _____ go back to that sin because if you go back to the same sin, it is an indication that you did not _____ repent"?

4) Also, what if someone commits a "_____" sin after he or she gets saved – a sin the person had never before committed? Does that person get _____, and does he or she now need to "turn from that sin" in order to get re-saved?

b. If repentance requires some level of improving one's spirituality by sinning _____, then one can see that this response is a _____ response requiring individuals to clean up their life in order to be saved or stay saved.

c. This puts the focus of repentance on a "change of _____" and NOT a "change of _____," which is a misuse of the word *repent*.

    d. This type of thinking _____ Biblical thinking. Biblical thinking = "I am a helpless sinner, and I _____ a Savior." Unbiblical thinking is associated with a change of conduct view of repentance = "I am a hopeful sinner, and I can _____ clean myself up."

    e. No amount of behavioral reform, character reform, education, commitment, or renouncement of sins can provide cleansing from the consequence of _____ sins! The "wages of sin is death," and Jesus Himself and He alone paid the penalty for your sins (including future sins) in _____ on the cross!

9. For a detailed look at multiple Bible passages and the meaning of the use of the word translated *repent* in those passages, see the "Extra Study" section for Lesson 6.

LESSON SEVEN

Gospel Response Clichés – (#8) Make Christ the Lord of Your
Life (i.e., Lordship Salvation)

A. **Quick Review**

1. Mankind's _____-fold problem is summarized as:
   (1) We have a _____ we cannot pay (death), AND
   (2) We do not have the _____ righteousness
   needed to enter Heaven (God's perfect place).

2. The gospel is the only thing that takes care of our
   _____-fold problem. The gospel is the only
   _____.

3. The gospel is the objective, historical message of
   what God has _____ done to save us from
   His just wrath (our debt) and provide us with a
   righteousness that we could never obtain ourselves,
   thereby enabling us to live eternally with Him.

4. What exactly did God do? He sent His Son Jesus
   Christ (fully God and fully man) to _____ for our
   sins and _____ again.

5. According to the Scriptures, there is only one
   response required of mankind. It is _____ alone
   in Christ alone. This is simply taking God at His
   Word and trusting in His _____ (Christ
   and His finished work) for our salvation.

B. Gospel Response Cliche #8: Make Christ the Lord of Your Life – Lordship Salvation

1. This is a cliché that uses Biblical terminology but, unfortunately, _____ justification with sanctification.

   a) Should believers _____ to the Lordship or mastery of Christ in their lives? 100%, yes!

   b) But, do unbelievers have to submit to the Lordship or mastery of Christ in their lives in order to be _____? No!

      1) Faith alone in the finished work of Christ alone is the _____ Biblical response required to be saved from the penalty of sin (death) and receive eternal life.

      2) The moment people add an _____ condition, including this gospel cliché of making Jesus the Lord of their lives, they have introduced a gospel *of works*.

2. Now, some additional, clarifying comments are in order because in order for an unbeliever to be saved, he or she has to have an _____ view of *Who* Jesus Christ is. Jesus is fully God and fully man! He is Lord!

   a. In Romans 10:9-10, notice that the unbeliever is not instructed to "make Jesus Lord of his or her life" but rather is told to "_____

Jesus as Lord."

1) Remember that the word *confess* means to
"say the _____ thing." The truth that
one must "say the same thing as" or "agree
with" the Lord Jesus. What does this mean
in context?

2) The Greek word *kurios* translated *Lord* has a
generic meaning of lord, master, owner, or
sir. It was generically a title of _____.

3) However, it came to have a more
_____ use, especially as it related to
the Greek translation of the Old Testament
(the Septuagint or LXX). This word *kurios* is
used of the covenant-keeping God of Israel
(_____or Jehovah) over 8,600 times!

4) These _____ Jews were to
confess that Jesus is God or Deity. They were
to _____ with Paul and the Word of
God that Jesus was Yahweh. (See John 8:24.)

b. The problem with the lordship gospel response
cliche is that it takes a _____
truth (submitting to Christ's Lordship) and
makes it a justification truth (how to get saved).

1) This "muddying of the waters"
_____ the 160 clear verses, which

give *faith* as the *ONLY* required response for justification. (See Appendix #2: 160 Verses Proving Justification by Faith Alone.)

2) It is interesting to note that when comparing Bible versions (KJV, NKJV, NASB, NIV, and ESV) that the word *surrender* is _____ found in a salvation context. In fact, the word is only used _____ in the NIV (Luke 23:25; 1 Corinthians 13:3) and _____ in the NASB (1 Corinthians 13:3).

   a) If *surrendering* to Christ were a _____ to be saved, shouldn't we expect it to be taught in the Bible?

   b) When looking at the words in the Bible translated as *commit* and *submit*, they, too, have no relevance to the topic of _____, but rather they relate to sanctification and other issues.

3) The lordship gospel response cliché requires a commitment to be _____ to Christ in your life as a definition of submission to Christ's lordship to be saved. However, no one could do this perfectly enough to warrant or _____ heaven.

c.   The lordship gospel response cliché could never allow anyone to know for sure he or she is saved, and thus their adherents lack _____.

1)   1 John 5:13 says, "These things I have written to you who believe in the name of the Son of God, that you may _____ that you have eternal life." God wants believers to *KNOW* that they have eternal life the _____ they believe, *NOT* after a lifetime of faithfulness.

2)   Who can claim that they have never at any point in time _____ Christ's Lordship in their life? In fact, Christians do this every time they sin.

3)   If this were the TRUE standard, or a requirement for salvation, then _____ _____ could ever be saved!

4)   In fact, what saves a person? A lifetime of _____ yielding to the Lord, or a Savior paying one's sin-debt in full, so that its penalty is _____ required of anyone personally? Clearly, the Bible teaches that it is the _____ work of Christ, which is designed to give a believer full assurance (Hebrews 10:1-14).

d. The lordship gospel response cliché does not
    recognize the Biblical reality of a _____
    Christian.

    1) To be clear at the outset, we would
        passionately argue that the Bible *DOES
        NOT* _____ carnality in the
        life of a believer; however, it does recognize
        the possibility of a believer living carnally.

    2) Lordship proponents teach that a *carnal*
        Christian ("one who is not _____
        submitted to the lordship of Christ"), is
        NOT a Christian at all.

        a) Lordship proponents say that this
            person was _____ really saved at
            all if he or she continues in unrepentant
            carnality.

        b) However, this is a perfect case of one's
            theology _____ one's
            interpretation.

    3) In 1 Corinthians 3:1-4, Paul specifically tells
        the   Corinthian   believers   that   they
        _____ *carnal.*

        a) Paul is speaking to _____ believers
            here. How do we know this? It is because
            in Chapter 3:1, Paul calls them *brethren.*

       i.   This is a term that Paul and other Biblical writers use to describe and address _____ in Jesus Christ.

      ii.   In fact, Paul uses the term *brethren* in _____ chapter of 1 Corinthians except chapter 13.

b) In chapter 3:3, Paul says the Corinthian believers are *still* carnal. This is an _____ condition that has persisted over some amount of time.

      i.   This statement indicates that carnality in the life of the believer can be in an _____ state. Again, this is NOT desirable or encouraged, but it is _____.

c) All the verbs in 3:3-4 are _____ tense verbs, indicating current or present action and even continual action. Thus, they were presently living in a _____ state of carnality.

e. The lordship gospel response cliché confuses the word _____ with _____ or *will* in the passages regarding sanctification.

1) Every orthodox Bible teacher would agree that believers *should not* live _____ in sin.

2) Unfortunately, those who teach this lordship gospel response cliché as a pre-requisite for salvation take it a step further when they say a *true* believer _____ habitually live in sin. In other words, they think it is an impossibility.

3) The very _____ of imperative commands in the New Testament imply that Christians *can* sin!

   a) If someone does *NOT* have the _____ to do something, then there is NO need to tell him or her not to do it!

   b) The very presence of the commands "not to sin" or not to "live continually in sin" tell us that believers have the _____ for doing so (Romans 6:12-13; Ephesians 4:17ff).

4) The use of the Greek _____ mood in sanctification passages is a strong argument against the *guaranteed* sanctification that the lordship gospel response cliché demands.

a) The Greek subjunctive mood is a mood that presents the verbal action as being _____or intentional. It can also express verbal action in terms of mere _____.

b) The Greek indicative mood is the mood in which the action of the verb is presented as real. It is the mood of assertion – asserting something as actual or _____.

c) Consider the following passages that teach the _____ concept (subjunctive mood) rather than the *will* or _____ concept (indicative mood).

   i. Romans 6:4, 12 – "Therefore we were buried with Him through baptism into death, that just as Christ was raised from the dead by the glory of the Father, even so we also *SHOULD WALK* in newness of life.... Therefore do not let sin reign in your mortal body, that you *SHOULD OBEY* it in its lust."

      a) This means that God _____ believers to

walk in newness of life, and they should not obey indwelling sin, but it means that it is *NOT* _____. Why? Because believers must choose to walk by faith in the finished work of Christ (our co-crucifixion and co-resurrection with Him) in order to benefit the deliverance from sin's power.

ii.   Ephesians 2:10 – "For we are His workmanship, created in Christ Jesus for good works, which God prepared beforehand that we *SHOULD WALK* [subjunctive mood] in them."

a)   This means that God _____ believers to walk in the good works He has prepared for them, but it also means that it is *NOT* _____. Why? Because believers must choose to walk by faith and respond to the Lord in order to execute these good works.

iii. Titus 2:12 – "Teaching us that, denying ungodliness and worldly lusts, we *SHOULD LIVE* [subjunctive mood] soberly, righteously, and godly in the present age."

   a) This means that grace _____ to teach believers to live soberly, righteously, and godly, but it is *NOT* _____. Why? Because believers must choose to walk by faith and respond to what grace is teaching them.

iv. Titus 3:8 – "This is a faithful saying, and these things I want you to affirm constantly, that those who have believed in God *SHOULD BE CAREFUL* [subjunctive mood] to maintain good works. These things are good and profitable to men."

   a) This means that God _____ for believers to maintain good works, but it is *NOT*

_____ that they will. Why? Because believers must choose to walk by faith and respond to Paul and Titus' continued encouragement and affirmation regarding these good works.

LESSON EIGHT

Gospel Response Clichés – (#9) Believe and Be Baptized in Water

A. Quick Review

1. Mankind's _____-fold problem is summarized as:
   (1) We have a _____we cannot pay (death), AND
   (2) We do not have the _____ righteousness
   needed to enter Heaven (God's perfect place).

2. The gospel is the only thing that takes care of our
   ___-fold problem. The gospel is the only _____.

3. The gospel is the objective, historical message of
   what God has _____ done to save us from
   His just wrath (our debt) and provide us with a
   righteousness that we could never obtain ourselves,
   thereby enabling us to live eternally with Him.

4. What exactly did God do? He sent His Son Jesus
   Christ (fully God and fully man) to _____ for
   our sins and _____ again.

5. According to the Scriptures, there is only one
   response required of man. It is _____ alone
   in Christ alone. This is simply taking God at His
   Word and trusting in His _____
   (Christ and His finished work) for our salvation.

B. Gospel Response Cliche #9: Believe and Be Baptized in Water – Baptismal Regeneration

1. Many of our gospel response cliches are Biblical concepts simply taught out of order. Water baptism is a great example of this because water baptism is designed to be a public _____ of salvation for believers, not the means of salvation for the unsaved.

2. What does the word *baptism* mean? It means to put into, to _____ with, to immerse, to be submerged, or to be placed in union with.

    a) The word was used the following ways in _____ culture: of soldiers dipping (*baptizo*) the tips of their spears in pigs' blood before battle; of a white cloth being immersed (*baptizo*) into a colored vat of dye; of a sinking ship or someone sinking in mud; of how a cucumber is made into a pickle.

    b) Please note that the word itself does *NOT* convey ____!

3. Some quick points to consider when seeing the word *baptism* in the Bible:

    a) Not all baptisms in the Bible are _____ baptisms, which involve water. In fact, there are *seven* different kinds of baptisms mentioned in the Bible and _____ of them are dry, and only three of them are wet! (***See Appendix 5 – Seven Baptisms of the Bible***)

b) Every time one runs into the word *baptism* in the Bible, one must remember the overall generic meaning of the word and try to understand the _____ in which it is being used.

c) There are 160 verses in the New Testament that teach that salvation is by faith _____ with *NO* mention of baptism as an additional pre-requisite *(See Appendix 2 – 160 Verses Proving Justification by Faith Alone).* Ephesians 2:8-9 specifically says that salvation is "not of works" and "not of yourselves."

   1. In contrast to the overwhelming Scriptural evidence that the only required response to the gospel is faith in the finished work of Christ alone, there are roughly _____ main passages that individuals will use to promote baptismal regeneration as an additional response. (*See the "Extra Study" for Lesson 8.*)

   2. Consider a logical argument though. If the Bible does not contradict itself, and we believe that it does not, which view has the greater burden of interpretative _____? (1) Holding to faith alone in Christ alone according to 160 Bible verses and then seeing how the seven verses (mentioned

above) _____ with the 160? OR (2)
Holding to belief plus baptism according to
the seven verses and then explaining how the
other 160 verses _____ with the seven verses?

d) Baptizing believers was not the _____ of
Jesus' ministry (John 4:1-2), nor Paul's ministry
(1 Corinthians 1:17) where he distinctly separates
baptism from *the gospel.*

e) Baptism is not mentioned as part of the gospel
_____ that Paul preached in
1 Corinthians 15:1-4.

f) If baptism were an _____ pre-requisite
for our salvation, then the salvation spoken of in
the Bible would be a works-salvation. In other
words, a required _____ or external
_____ of our own doing would be required.
However, this would be in direct contradiction
with Romans 4:5, which says, "But to him who
DOES NOT work but believes on Him ..."

g) Water baptism does not do something _____
you, but rather it reflects something already done
_____ you. In this sense, it is a visual aid of our
already _____ spiritual baptism
into Christ (1 Corinthians 12:13; Romans 6:3-4).

4. What went wrong with the meaning of the word *baptism*, and why is its meaning so jumbled and confusing today?

   a) From an early period in church history (the second century), baptism began to be more _____. Additionally, it came to be seen as having a mystical quality to it. People begin to mention prayer to *sanctify* the water. Thus, from the end of the second century on, it was widely believed that baptism washed away _____.

   b) It was also around this time that candidates for baptism often had a three-year _____ period to see if their conversion was legitimate and if their _____ had truly changed. If they made it through these three years, then they were instructed in Christian doctrine, made to memorize a "creed" of some sort, and then baptized.

   c) The almost universal mode of baptism at this time was usually full _____ in a river or a bathhouse of a large house. At their baptism, candidates answered questions about their beliefs in the Trinity and were dunked _____ times.

   d) Eventually, tradition required a church _____ to lay hands on the person

being baptized, and even later the church leader
began to pray for the believer to _____
the Holy Spirit at baptism.

e) Other factors, which played into the confusion
regarding baptismal regeneration, were
Augustine's teaching on _____ sin and the
high infant mortality rate during this time in
history. Because of these two factors, infant
baptism began to be widespread by the middle
of the fourth century. It was taught that baptism
washed away _____ sin.

f) Thus, by the sixth century, the _____
baptisms being done were infant baptisms, and
we had a "Christian" world.

5. Biblically speaking, water baptism was given to the
disciples of Jesus Christ as one _____ of
making additional disciples. Turn to Matthew 28:18-
20 – the Great Commission.

a) In this passage, there is one main verb (an
imperative _____) with three
participles, which modify the main verb. These
three participles further describe _____ you
would do the action of the main verb!

1) "Make disciples" is our main verb, and it is
the _____ command in this passage.
This verb means to not only learn, but to

become a follower of one's teacher in both doctrine and conduct of life.

2) "Go," or better said "as you are going," is the first participle _____ this verb. Thus, disciple-making is to happen as the disciples went from one place to another in their daily lives.

3) "Teaching" is the second participle modifying this verb. They were to teach their disciples to observe all the things that Jesus Christ commanded His original disciples.

   a) This could involve _____, systematized study of sorts, but it could also include personal Biblical instruction regarding life issues.

   b) This is where the disciple-maker utilizes the divine _____ that God has given him or her through years of spiritual growth to instruct those he or she is discipling as they navigate life.

4) "Baptizing" is the third participle modifying this verb. They were to baptize their disciples in water, "in the name of the Father, and of the Son, and of the Holy Spirit."

   a) This   was   a   public _____ with

Jesus Christ and His message of faith-righteousness.

b) This, too, was a _____ aid of the truth that became true of them the moment they believed. The Spirit of God identified, or baptized, the believer into the body of Christ (1 Corinthians 12:13).

c) This truth was hopefully in the forefront of the disciples' mind when they agreed to be water baptized, and thus the *teaching* aspect   of   discipleship _____ nicely with the water baptism aspect.

6. For a detailed look at the seven Bible passages that purport to teach the doctrine of baptismal regeneration, see the "Extra Study" section for Lesson 8.

LESSON FOUR – EXTRA STUDY

(continuation of outline from Lesson Four)

    b. 2 Timothy 2:11-13

        1) Paul uses the same grammatical structure for each of these conditional statements. They are all first-class _____ statements in Greek.

        2) First-class conditional statements _____ the fulfillment of the condition for argument's sake. In other words, you could say, "If THIS is true, and let's assume that it is for argument's sake, then THAT will happen."

        3) So, in verse 11, it would read, "If we died with Christ, and let's _____ that we did die with Christ for argument's sake, (then) we shall also live with Him."

           a) Do believers indeed die _____ Christ? Yes, this truth is taught all over the Scriptures (Romans 6:1-11; Colossians 2:20-3:4; Galatians 2:20).

           b) The

_____

then is that believers will indeed live with

Him. This guarantee is made even more certain using the future indicative for the word *live*. The future indicative represents a guaranteed _____.

4) Thus, in verse 12a, it would read, "If we endure, and let's _____ that we will for argument's sake, (then) we shall also reign with Him."

   a) The word *endure* means to remain _____, to persevere, or to bear up under.

   b) James uses this same word (in noun form) in James 1:3-4 as something that is *produced* or *grows* through the process of trials, which indicates that *enduring* is something that is not done _____ or consistently throughout a believer's life.

   c) As a born-again believer lives faithfully in life through different trials, trusting the Lord, they will have a more privileged position or role in the future _____ of Christ's kingdom.

d) At some level, each believer will
_____, and thus at some level the
believer will reign with Christ. This is
guaranteed! The level at which each
believer endures is based _____
on his or her repeated responses of faith
during trials.

5) Therefore, in verse 12b, it would read, "If we
deny Him, and let's _____ that
we will for argument's sake, (then) He also
will deny us."

a) Now, since this is assumed to be true of
all believers, if this denial of us by Jesus
Christ reflected a _____ of
salvation, then how could anyone be
saved? So, what exactly is Christ
_____ the believer
who denies Him?

b) Because of the emphasis in this passage
on living faithfully while enduring
potential hardship, and because of the
previous statement in verse 12a about
reigning with Him, it seems best to
understand this denial as a denial of
future _____.

    c) Every time a believer sins either explicitly (by being ashamed of and denying Jesus Christ _____) or implicitly (by sinning in general, as this constitutes a rejection or denial of Jesus Christ), the believer is effectively missing out on _____ reward.

6) In verse 13, it would also read, "If we are faithless, and let's assume that we will be for argument's sake, (then) He remains faithful; He cannot deny Himself."

    a) So, regarding the believer's unfaithful action (a sin) or ongoing state of actions (habitual sin), this verse makes two _____ statements about God's character.

    b) **First**, "He remains faithful to the believer." This is God's abiding state of response to the believer, regardless of how the believer is _____ responding to the Lord.

    c) **Second**, "He cannot deny Himself." Notice, it does not say that God *cannot deny the believer* but rather that He *cannot deny* _____. How would

God be denying Himself if He did not
remain faithful to the believer?

i. He would be denying/rejecting His
    _____, such as no death penalty,
    eternal life, forgiveness of sins,
    building His Church, etc.

ii. He would be denying/rejecting the
    finished _____ of Christ and
    the _____ of what
    He accomplished.

iii. He would be denying/rejecting His
    own _____ of
    truthfulness and omniscience.

iv. He would be denying/rejecting the
    believer's very _____
    with His Son because the believer is
    inextricably unified with Jesus Christ.

LESSON SIX – EXTRA STUDY

(continuation of outline from Lesson Six)

9. Consider the following passages in _____ and determine what the author/speaker is instructing his audience to change their minds about:

   a. Matthew 3:2-11 – What was John the Baptist instructing his _____ to change their minds about?

      1) About the _____ needed to enter the Kingdom of God. John's Jewish audience believed that since they were physical descendants of Abraham, Isaac, and Jacob as well as circumcised, they would get into the Kingdom (3:9).

      2) Paul made clear what John the Baptist preached, and what he _____ when he used the word *repent* in Acts 19:4. John wanted people to *change their minds* about what they were _____ in to get into the Kingdom, and he wanted them to put their trust in Jesus Christ alone for a right standing with God.

   b. Acts 2:38 – What was Peter instructing his _____ to change their minds about?

1) About the _____ of Jesus Christ. Fifty days earlier, the Jewish people determined that Jesus was worthy of a criminal's death.

2) Peter wanted them to change their minds about Jesus Christ – that He was *NOT* _____ of death. He was their Messiah and worthy of their trust and worship.

c. Acts 17:30-31 – What was Paul instructing his _____ to change their minds about?

1) About their _____ to the one true God. Paul was addressing a Gentile, pagan, and polytheistic audience in Athens. They were very superstitious and worshipped many false gods, largely due to fear of upsetting any of them.

2) Paul commanded them to *change their* _____." WHY? Because of what verse 31, which says, "Because He has appointed a day on which He will judge the world in righteousness by the Man whom He has ordained. He has given assurance of this to all by raising Him from the dead."

3) These pagan polytheists needed to stop worrying about what the false gods *might* do to them and _____ in the one true God who provided the _____ of

escape from judgment. They needed to change their minds.

d. Acts 20:21 – What was Paul instructing his

_____ to change their minds about?

1) Paul has _____ audiences mentioned here. *First*, his Jewish audience, who needed to change their minds about _____ Jesus Christ is and put their faith in Him alone for salvation/righteousness. (See Acts 2:38)

2) *Second*, Paul's Gentile audience, who needed to change their minds about _____ and put their faith in the one true God alone and His solution – Jesus Christ and His finished work on the cross – for their sin problem. (See Acts 17:30-31.)

e. Acts 26:20 – What was Paul instructing his

_____ to change their minds about?

1) Although not given in detail in this passage, Paul mentions both Jew and Gentile, so it is most likely the same *change of mind* described in the previous passages (Acts 2:38; 17:30-31; 20:21).

2) What is even more fascinating about this passage is the distinction provided between the words _____ and

_____ *to God* AND *repent*

and *doing* _____ *befitting repentance.*

a) The first comparison this communicates is that repentance is different and _____ from *turning to God.* They   are   *NOT* _____!

Repentance can (and should) lead to turning to God, but it is *NOT* synonymous, nor guaranteed.

b) The second comparison this reveals is that repentance is different and _____ from *doing works.* In other words, repentance is a change of mind, whereas *doing works* is a change of _____.

Repentance can (and should) lead to a lifestyle of *doing works*, but it is *NOT* synonymous, nor guaranteed.

LESSON EIGHT – EXTRA STUDY

(continuation of outline from Lesson Eight)

6. So, let's consider the seven passages that purport to teach the doctrine of baptismal regeneration:

   a. **#1: Ephesians 4:5** – "One Lord, one faith, one baptism ...."

      1) As mentioned earlier, the Bible describes _____ different baptisms, so to which baptism does this verse refer? It refers to the *one* baptism that *ALL* believers have in _____, which is the baptism that put them *IN* Christ by the Holy Spirit. (See 1 Corinthians 12:13.)

      2) What is referred to in Ephesians 4:5 is _____ baptism (dry) *NOT* water baptism (wet). This is the *only* baptism that ALL believers have in _____ because this baptism happens _____ to individuals when they put their faith in Jesus Christ alone for salvation.

      3) Notice the following in 1 Corinthians 12:13, which connects us to Ephesians 4:5 and its emphasis of unity:

a) The use of the word *ALL* _____ times describing *ALL* believers – "We were *ALL* baptized...." and "... have ALL been made to drink...."

b) The use of the word *ONE* _____ times – "We were all baptized into *ONE* body...." and "... have all been made to drink into *ONE* Spirit..."

c) The _____ of the *ONEs* in both 1 Corinthians 12:13 and Ephesians 4:4-5 – *ONE* body and *ONE* Spirit.

d) Also, notice the connection between 1 Corinthians 12:13 and Ephesians (in general) in that they mention that this spiritual baptism is the thing that _____ Jews and Greeks and slaves and free in the body of Christ.

b. ***#2: Mark 16:16*** – "He who believes and is baptized will be saved; but he who does not believe will be condemned."

1) Let's consider some key points of _____ for this verse.

a) Mark 16:9-15 are facts _____ in the other Biblical Gospel accounts.

b) This passage in Mark is *his* version of the
_____ Commission, which we
also find in Matthew's account in chapter
28:19-20.

c) One minor _____
between the two Great Commissions
found in Mark and Matthew is that the
word *preach* is the one command in Mark,
whereas "*make disciples*" is the one
command in Matthew 28.

d) From Matthew's account, it is clear that
part of being a _____ of
Jesus Christ involves being water
baptized. "*Baptizing them*" is a participle
of means, describing _____
one makes disciples. It is through water
baptism (public identification with Jesus
Christ) and through teaching them to
observe all the things that Jesus had
commanded them.

2) Having considered the context, what now is
Mark 16:15-16 _____?

a) ***First***, the phrase "*is baptized*" is in the
passive voice, which requires
_____ _____ to
complete the action on the person who

believes. In other words, according to someone who holds the baptismal regeneration view, one cannot be saved unless another person is _____ to baptize him or her.

b) So, hypothetically, if a person were to put his or her trust in Christ alone, but he or she was _____ with no exposure to another human being, God could not save the person. By definition, this would require _____ _____ Jesus Christ's finished work alone, *AND* it would require another human being to secure a person's salvation.

c) ***Second***, if we are just looking at the _____, what is/are the condition(s) of being _____ in verse 16? *Believe* and *be baptized.*

d) ***Third,*** if we are just looking at the _____, what is/are the condition(s) of being _____ in verse 16? *Not believing.* Notice that *not* being baptized is *not* mentioned.

i.   To use an example, it is like saying that he (any person) who gets on a bus and sits down will go to New York. That does not mean that one must _____ _____ in order to get to New York. Technically, all that is necessary to get to New York is to get on the bus.

ii.   So, in Mark 16:16 and bringing this illustration home, *believing* is getting on the _____, whereas *being baptized* is _____ _____ in the seat provided.

iii.   What God ultimately desires is that each person trusts in Jesus Christ alone for his or her salvation, *AND* that he or she continues walking with Him in _____ throughout one's life. However, walking with Him in discipleship is *NOT* a _____ for being saved or being born again.

e)   Fourth, consider how Jesus finishes His statement in Mark 16. He describes certain signs that will follow _____ people, but notice HOW He describes a saved

individual – "those who believe."
_____, "those who believe *AND* are baptized!"

    i.   Again, when we really study the pre-requisite for salvation, notice that being baptized is _____ a couple of times in this passage in Mark and *NOT* mentioned as a pre-requisite the 160 other times in the New Testament.

c.   ***#3: Galatians 3:27*** – "For as many of you as were baptized into Christ have put on Christ."

   1)   Let's consider some key points of _____ for this verse.

      a)   Galatians 3 is about the proper _____ of the law in relation to salvation, namely our justification before God. Paul's emphasis is that believers are justified (declared righteous) by faith _____ without any effort or ability required to keep the law.

         i.   In fact, the irony of using this passage to teach baptismal _____ is that Paul is making the strongest argument possible in this passage *against* any other   response   except   faith

_____.

ii.   In a book designed to clarify the
gospel message, it is ironic that the
word *baptism* (noun form) and the
word *baptized* (verb form) are only
used _____ – in verse 27.

b) In this passage, Paul is in the middle of
using common, modern-day _____
of a child coming to maturity to reflect
the believer's new position in Christ.

i.   ***First***, the need for a _____ while
a child is in his or her pre-adolescent
years. The role of a tutor was to
guide the child to and from school
and home. Once the child was an
adult and a mature son, the tutor was
no longer needed (3:23-25).

ii.   ***Second***,   the   picture   of
_____, or becoming a full
son with inheritance rights, is
communicated via the use of the
Greek word *huios*, translated "son" in
verse 26 and the description of
adoption that follows in 4:1-2.

     iii.   ***Third***, the imagery utilized in the phrase "putting on" Christ seems to continue the imagery of a child coming to maturity by subtly referencing the practice of providing a young man a new piece of clothing (an adult _____) when they reached *son* status (3:27).

2) Having now considered the context, what is Galatians 3:27 teaching?

    a) Notice, first of all, that the verse does *NOT* say "baptized into water" or even simply "baptized," but it specifically says, "baptized into Christ." This is speaking of _____ baptism, as referenced in 1 Corinthians 12:13.

        i.   The same phrase "baptized into" is used in Romans 6:3 of being baptized into Christ's _____, in 1 Corinthians 10:2 of being baptized into _____, and in 1 Corinthians 12:13 of being baptized into One _____ (the Church).

        ii.   All these are _____ baptisms, and all the *dry* baptisms in the Bible are spiritual baptisms, not involving water or other _____.

b) So, how do we get *into Christ*? Is it through water baptism or dry baptism, and how do we _____ for sure? 1 Corinthians 1:30 tells us the following: "... but of Him [God the Father] you are in Christ Jesus..."

c) So, we get *into* Christ not through a water baptism by _____, but via spiritual baptism by _____ the Holy Spirit (1 Corinthians 12:13).

d) Paul is simply making an argument that if you have believed in the Lord Jesus Christ, then you have been _____ by the Spirit of God *into* Him. Thus, you have "put on" Christ, reflecting sonship and the full inheritance that comes with that designation.

d. **_#4: John 3:5_** – "Jesus answered, 'Most assuredly, I say to you, unless one is born of water and the Spirit, he cannot enter the kingdom of God.'"

1) Let's consider some key points of _____ for this verse.

a) Jesus is in the middle of a conversation with Nicodemus, a highly esteemed Jewish religious leader, involving the _____ of the new birth to enter God's Kingdom (the eternal state).

b) Jesus' use of the phrase "you must be born again" or "born from above" seems to really _____ Nicodemus, as evidenced by his initial response to Jesus in 3:4.

c) So, Jesus' answer in verses 5-8 is designed to further explain to Nicodemus the concept of being "born again," and Jesus seems _____ that His explanation does not help Nicodemus' understanding (3:10).

   i.   Jesus expects Nicodemus to understand His _____, as He says, "Are you the teacher of Israel, and do not know these things?"

   ii. It is this question that gives us an idea of where Jesus had taken Nicodemus in verses 5-8 to _____ the concept of being "born again." Jesus was using examples of new birth as described

in the _____ Testament!

2) Having now considered the context, what is

John 3:5 teaching?

a) Starting in verse 5, Jesus uses three

_____ examples from the Old

Testament that Nicodemus should have

known since he was a preeminent

_____ in the nation of Israel (3:10).

b) At first _____, the two phrases

"born of water" and "(born of) the

Spirit" seem to be two separate phrases

and two distinct events.

   i. However, the preposition *OF*

   governs _____ water and

   Spirit, meaning that both terms are a

   description of the _____ thing

   (one's spiritual birth).

   ii. It seems as if, in this verse, Jesus is

   indirectly referring Nicodemus to

   Ezekiel 36 and the

   _____ of Israel, via

   the New Covenant, when Israel

   enters the Millennial Kingdom.

   iii. In Ezekiel 36:25-28, Ezekiel mentions both *water* and the *spirit* with the _____ birth.

   iv. Ezekiel 36:25 – God would sprinkle clean _____ on them, and they will be clean; He (God) would cleanse them from all their filthiness and from all their idols.

   v. Ezekiel 36:26-27 – God would give them a new _____ within them and cause them to walk in His statues, so that they would be able to keep His judgments and do them.

   vi. Ezekiel 36:28 – Then, and only then, they *will dwell* (_____ and live) in the land that He gave to their fathers; they shall be His people, and He will be their God.

c) In John 3:6, Jesus distinguishes spiritual birth from fleshly birth by alluding to the _____ birth of Isaac in contrast to Ishmael. This story should have reminded Nicodemus that physical birth was *NOT* enough to be a son of the promised covenant.

d) In John 3:8, Jesus alludes to Ezekiel 37:1-14 where the Spirit of God brought life to a valley full of dead _____, and where _____ is associated with the life that the Spirit breathed into these bones.

e. **#5: Acts 2:38** – "Then Peter said to them, 'Repent, and let every one of you be baptized in the name of Jesus Christ for the remission of sins; and you shall receive the gift of the Holy Spirit.'"

  1) Consider some key points of _____ for this verse.

    a) The Day of Pentecost had come, and the Holy Spirit had _____ from Heaven, as promised by Jesus Christ, to indwell believers.

    b) As a sign to _____ their new message, the believers indwelt with the Holy Spirit spoke in languages, which were up until that moment unfamiliar to them.

    c) All the traveling Jews, who were in town for the Feasts of Passover and Pentecost, heard their own native dialects in the gift of _____, declaring the "wonderful works of God" (2:11).

d) The Jewish crowd present accused the men of being _____ with wine, which Peter corrects and rightly communicates that these men are actually filled with the Holy Spirit, which is similar to what the Lord will do at a _____ date in the last days during the Tribulation Period (Joel 2:28-32).

   i.   The similarity between Acts 2 and Joel 2, which Peter is recognizing, is the _____ of the Holy Spirit, resulting in unusual manifestations, but it is very much different and not the same event.

e) Peter has just preached a _____, which starts at verse 22 and culminates in verse 36.

f) His sermon reviewed the history of Jesus, reminded the men of what they had seen and witnessed, explained that the indwelling Holy Spirit was a promise from God, tied in Old Testament passages that applied to Jesus' resurrection (as communicated through

David), identified Jesus as Israel's long-awaited Messiah, and put the full _____ on the men listening, telling them that they crucified Him. He concludes the sermon in verse 36 by letting the audience know that God made Jesus both Lord and Christ.

g) In response to Peter's sermon, the men ask in verse 37, "What shall we do?" They had recognized that they had made a _____ and wanted to know if there was anything they could do to escape _____ from God on the basis of crucifying Jesus.

    i. The pending judgment on the Jewish nation was often announced by the presence of foreign _____ in Jerusalem. (See Isaiah 28:11; Also, 1 Corinthians 14:21 ties this in with the purpose of the spiritual gift of tongues/languages.)

2) Having now considered the big picture context, consider some additional _____ that will be helpful before we dive into the details of Acts 2:38.

a) We know from history that Luke wrote the Gospel of Luke and the Book of Acts as a kind of two-volume church _____ set. The first volume recorded the events of the life of Jesus Christ, and the second volume followed up on the events surrounding His earliest followers.

b) Luke's version or recording of the Great Commission is found in Luke 24:46-47, which reads, "Then He said to them, 'Thus it is written, and thus it was necessary for the Christ to suffer and to rise from the dead the third day, and that _____ and remission of sins should be preached in His name to all nations, beginning at Jerusalem.'"

  i. Notice the use of the phrase "repentance and remission of sins" in Luke's _____ Commission account.

  ii. Notice what Peter preaches in Acts 2:38 – "_____ and remission of sins." Peter also does so in Acts 3:19 when he says, "_____ therefore and be converted, that your sins may be *blotted out* [used in place of remission of sins]" and in Acts 5:31 when he says, "… to give _____ to Israel and forgiveness of sins."

iii. If one were to look at what _____ *repentance* in each of these passages in Acts, one will notice an accusation against the audience's _____ in the murder of Jesus. This is WHAT they needed *to repent* (change their minds) of – the identity of Jesus Christ.

c) Interestingly enough, notice what is _____ from Luke 24:46-47 (Luke's Great Commission), Acts 3:19, and Acts 5:31. _____ is absent from all these passages.

d) One other thing to consider before we dive into Acts 2:38 is the use of the word *faith* with the phrase, *remission of sins,* in the Book of Acts. In fact, faith is clearly given as the _____ pre-requisite for receiving the *remission of sins.*

i.   Peter, in his sermon to Cornelius and his household, uses the phrase *remission of sins* in Acts 10:43. He also gives *faith* as the _____ requirement to obtain it.

ii. In Acts 11:17-18, Peter gives his own commentary on both the Gentile conversion and the events in Acts 2. He clearly states that the _____ requirement for receiving the gift of the Holy Spirit and eternal life is *believing on the Lord Jesus Christ.*

iii. Later, in Acts 13:38-39, the apostle Paul preaches a message at Antioch in Pisidia where he, too, gives faith as the _____ pre-requisite for the *forgiveness of sins.*

iv. At the Jerusalem council, which is recorded in Acts 15:7-11, Peter once again links both the Gentiles' initial conversion in Acts 10 and the Jews' initial conversion in Acts 2 with a response of faith _____. This response then results in the reception of the Holy Spirit and the remission of sins. Once again, there is **NO** mention of water baptism.

3) Having now looked at the full _____, what is Acts 2:38 teaching?

a) Notice the question in Acts 2:37 – "What shall *we* **do**?" – compared to the one in Acts 16:30 – "What must *I* do to be saved?"

    i. Paul's answer to the Philippian jailor's question in Acts 16:30 is found in Acts 16:31, where he replies, "_____ on the Lord Jesus Christ, and you will be saved, you and your household."

b) Because Peter's audience's question was _____ and open-ended, and because Peter was following the Great Commission prescription received from Christ only a _____ days or weeks earlier, "repentance and remission of sins" *and* "believer's baptism" were given in response.

    i. Peter basically responds to their broad and open-ended question with a _____ response – "Repent/rely upon the name of Jesus Christ"

PLUS "Be baptized" (what they must do as _____ of Christ after saving faith to publicly identify with Christ).

ii.   The Great Commission gave the full, _____ instruction on what the apostles were to do in building the Lord's Church: 1. Preach the gospel, *and* 2. _____ those who believe through baptizing them and teaching them. (See Matthew 28:19-20; Mark 16:15-16; Luke 24:46-47.)

c) The word *repent* is the Greek word *metanoeo*, which means a *change of mind*. The verb is used as an Aorist, Active, Imperative, 2nd person, _____.

d) *Baptize* is the Greek verb *baptize*, and it means *to immerse, to submerge, and to be identified with*. This verb is used as an Aorist, Passive, Imperative, 3rd person, _____.

e) Giving a literal translation, it is saying, "_____ of you need to repent, and _____ who repents needs to be baptized."

f) Additionally, notice the word order and use of the Greek _____ *epi*, translated as the word *in.*

    i.   The Greek word *epi* means *on, upon,* _____ *upon, upon the ground of, or upon the authority of.*

    ii.   A.T. Robertson, considered by many to be the Dean of American Biblical-Greek scholars, says of the "ground-meaning" (his words), "It is 'upon' .... '*epi*' implies a real _____ upon..."

    iii.   Notice the text does *NOT* say, "Repent and be baptized for the remission of your sins" but rather "Repent and be baptized in [_____ upon] the name of Jesus Christ for the remission of your sins."

4) Simply put and bringing it all together, Peter is simply telling his audience that they must _____ their minds about Jesus Christ (who He is, and what He has accomplished), rest upon Him by faith for remission of sins, and follow Him in

_____ through water

baptism, which is a public identification with

the Person and message of Jesus Christ.

f.   **#6: *Acts 22:16*** – "And now why are you waiting?

Arise and be baptized, and wash away your sins,

calling on the name of the Lord."

1) Consider   some   key   points   of

_____ for this verse.

a) This is one of three accounts of Paul's

_____ found in the Book of

Acts. Acts 9 (when Paul's conversion

happened), Acts 22 (Paul recounts the

events to a Jewish audience/mob at the

Temple), Acts 26 (Paul recounts the

events to King Agrippa, the great

grandson of Herod the Great).

b) (Acts 21:17-24): Leading up to this event,

Paul was instructed by James and the

elders of the church at Jerusalem to go to

the temple to make peace because Jews

everywhere thought Paul was teaching

_____ the Law and against

Moses. This was an especially sensitive

situation for local Jewish Christians.

c) (Acts 21:27-32): Jews from Asia (the

Ephesus area) recognize Paul in the

temple and go _____. They make accusations against Paul, saying that he taught against the "people, the law, and this place (the temple)." They also accuse him of bringing a Gentile (Trophimus the Ephesian) into a _____ area of the temple for Gentiles. As a result, the Jews in the temple seize him and plan to beat him to death.

d) (Acts 21:33-40): The Romans come in to break up the mob, and then Paul, once out of the grasp of the Jews, seeks to _____ the mob, and he does so in the Hebrew language. This catches the crowd off guard and gets their attention, and they begin to listen to Paul's testimony.

e) A lot of the facts of Paul's testimony are repeated verbatim in each story, but what is communicated in Acts 22:16 is _____ found in this account.

2) Having now looked at the context, what is Acts 22:16 _____?

a) The first question we must ask concerning Paul's testimony is: At what point in the narrative was Paul saved? Was he saved on the road to Damascus _____ Ananias arrived, or was he saved in the city of Damascus _____ Ananias arrived?

i.   Based upon the clear statements from the _____ accounts, it seems probable that Paul was saved before Ananias arrived on the scene.

ii.   Jesus refers to Paul as if he is _____ saved in Acts 9:12-15 when He calls Paul a "chosen vessel of Mine to bear My name before Gentiles, kings, and the children of Israel" and in Acts 22:10 when He tells Paul that He will tell him "all things which are _____ for you to do."

iii. Ananias refers to Paul as "_____ Saul" in both Acts 9:17 and Acts 22:13.

iv.   We also see that Paul received the Holy Spirit _____ he was baptized by water in Acts 9:17-18.

b) Ananias asks Paul a very pointed question to which he then provides some very pointed instructions – "And now why are you waiting?" The Greek word *mello* means *to wait or delay*. It describes a person who is _____ time unduly with the implication of a lack of decision.

   i.   Paul must have been in _____ at some level. Just three days earlier, he was going to Damascus to persecute Christians. He hated Christians, and he had this incredible experience on the road, lost his eyesight, and probably began to realize that his life was about to change. The uncertainty of it all at this moment must have _____ him.

c) Ananias wants to move Paul forward, and he gives Paul two specific _____: (1) be baptized, and (2) wash away your sins.

d) Additionally, Ananias gives Paul two _____ to modify the two commands. These are the following: (1) arise, and (2) call on the name of the

Lord. Let's consider the grammar of these words.

i. First, we must recognize which command goes with which participle. The command *to be baptized* is _____ with the participle *arise*. The command *to wash away your sins* is _____ with the participle *calling on the name of the Lord.*

ii. Second, the word *arise* is an aorist, active participle that is connected to the command *to be baptized*, which is an aorist, middle imperative. Grammatically, this tells us that you must *arise* _____ and then *be baptized*. One could say, "Having arisen, be baptized."

iii. Third, "calling on the name of the Lord" is an aorist, middle participle that is connected to the command *to wash away your sins,* which is an aorist, middle imperative. Grammatically, this tells us that you must *call on the name of the Lord* _____ and then *wash away your sins*. One could say, "Having called on the name of the Lord, wash away your sins."

e) Now, what does Ananias mean by telling Paul to "wash away your sins"? Is he telling Paul to get saved, or if Paul is _____ saved (as discussed earlier), could he be saying something else?

  i. Christians became known as those who *called upon* the name of the Lord Jesus Christ (Acts 9:14, 21; 1 Cor. 1:2). Christians recognized a higher authority than Caesar and a greater throne than his. They were citizens of a Heavenly city; and just as the Roman citizen appealed over the head of subordinate judges, so Christians _____ over the head of every earthly judge to the Judge of all. Their Lord and Savior sat on the right hand of the Majesty on High. Thus, "calling on the name of the Lord" is viewed as a characteristic activity of _____, *NOT* unbelievers.

  ii. Consider the order of Romans 10:13-15. Working backwards in the text but in chronological order: (1) preacher sent, (2) preacher preaches (3) people hear message, (4) people _____ message, and (5) people call upon the name of the Lord.

iii. The phrase "wash away your sins" is only used _____ other time in the New Testament. It is in 1 Corinthians 6:11, when in reference to the Corinthian believers, Paul says, "They were washed." Grammatically, this phrase in 1 Corinthians 6:11 is also found in the aorist, middle indicative like our Acts 22:16 usage. Interestingly enough, the other two phrases mentioned in 1 Corinthians 6:11 ("you were sanctified," and "you were justified") are both in the aorist, passive indicative. So, what is significant about the aorist, middle construction?

iv. The middle voice in Greek signifies that the subject of the verb is being _____ by its own action or is acting upon itself. The

New Testament often has human beings taking an action that has results that come back on us, but ultimately it is _____ who does the work. For example, (1) Romans 6:11 says that we are *to consider/reckon* ourselves dead to sin and alive to God. This is a present, middle imperative. But, *being dead to sin and alive to God* is God's doing, and our *reckoning/considering* (with a middle voice) is an act of faith that puts us in a position to _____ from God's doing. (2) In John 18:25, Peter was *warming* himself by the fire. This is a present, middle participle. Even though Peter is describing as doing the action, he was not the _____ of warming, since it was the fire. Still, he stood in such a way and in such a place as to be warmed by the doing of the fire.

v. So, what was Paul doing when he was calling on the name of the Lord to wash away his sins? It seems most likely, because of the timing of this exhortation (following His salvation), that this was more for _____ and moving forward with the Lord.

vi. Paul seemed to be struggling with his _____ regarding his former sins (Acts 22:19-20), and thus this was Ananias' way of encouraging him to move forward.

f) So, why is baptism commanded here if it is not for salvation? Again, it is the fulfillment of the _____ Commission, and the apostles/disciples took it very seriously.

i. When a Jew _____ identified himself with Jesus Christ as Messiah, it was a *big* deal, which impacted his or her current and future relationships with family, friends, business colleagues, and opportunities.

g. **#7: 1 Peter 3:20-21** – "… who formerly were disobedient, when once the Divine longsuffering waited in the days of Noah, while the ark was being prepared, in which a few, that is, eight souls, were saved through water. There is also an antitype which now saves us – baptism (not the removal of the filth of the flesh, but the answer of a good conscience toward God), through the resurrection of Jesus Christ."

1) Consider some key points of _____ for this verse.

   a) 1 Peter deals with a group of believers who are facing _____ for their faith. Most of the book weaves in and out of the topic of handling *suffering/persecution.*

   b) In chapter 3, starting in verse 13, Peter once again addresses the subject of _____, and once again he points to the example of Jesus Christ in verse 18. (See also 1 Peter 2:21-25.)

   c) Specifically, from verse 13 and following, Peter addresses the concept of suffering _____ (for righteousness' sake), and he uses Noah as an example of unjust suffering.

   d) Additionally, Peter uses Noah and the ark as an example of the Lord's _____ in judging sinners, meaning that God gives ample time for sinners to hear a message and then change their minds.

e) Peter basically says this to his _____ audience: "God is doing much bigger things in this life and through these trials than just trying to make your lives easy circumstantially (i.e., removing all trials, persecution, and tribulations)."

f) Believers are sharing in the suffering of Christ, and unbelievers are being given a chance to _____ to the gospel message through believer's actions/responses (verses 13-17).

g) So, the main theme in suffering is that *God wins!* Even though Christ may have suffered unjustly, verse 22 tells us that He is now exalted. Thus, the exhortation is to _____ God in the midst of suffering because He will sort out all punishment and reward.

2) Having now considered the bigger picture context of 1 Peter and our passage, consider some _____ context from Genesis and the story of Noah that will be

helpful before we dive into the details of 1 Peter 3:20-21.

a) The people in Noah's day were _____ (Gen 6:5, 11-12), but Noah found grace in the eyes of the Lord (Gen 6:8).

b) God commanded Noah to build an ark, and He gave him _____ instructions on how to build, and who/what to bring on board (Gen 6:14ff). Noah obeyed Him and followed His instructions to a T (Gen 6:22).

c) However, lest we solely emphasize Noah's *obedience*, Hebrews 11:7 sheds light on the _____ of his obedience, which was his faith. Now, let's ask and answer some questions based on Hebrews 11:7.

   i.   What saved Noah's household? The _____

   ii. What condemned the world? Noah's _____ of the Ark and the _____ of his preaching during his physical preparation of the Ark for 120 years (implied in the passage). Genesis 6:3

gives us the timeframe of 120 years, and 2 Peter 2:5 calls Noah a "preacher of righteousness."

iii. How did Noah become the "heir of righteousness?" Noah's preparation of the Ark, which _____ his faith. Noah carried on the mantle of *faith-righteousness* from Abel.

d) God sent the flood waters from above and beneath (Genesis 7:11), and God was the One who _____ them in the Ark (Genesis 7:16).

e) Three quick questions: (1) Who was saved from the flood? Those who were _____ the Ark. (2) Who was destroyed by the flood? Those who were *not* in the _____. (3) How were they destroyed? By the flood (by _____).

3) Having now looked at the _____ context, what is 1 Peter 3:20-21 teaching?

a) First, we have to address one phrase from verse 19, where it is says that Christ went and "_____ to the spirits in prison," who "formerly were disobedient" in Noah's day.

i.   These *spirits* are the spirits of
_____ in Noah's day,
who had rejected his preaching and
the visual aid of the construction of
the Ark.

ii.   Christ, through the Holy Spirit,
preached _____ Noah (2
Peter 2:5) to these men and women
while they were on earth.

b) *Verse 20*: With these people God was
very _____ in Noah's day. In
fact, God's *longsuffering* is emphasized
regarding the persecution of Noah and
the rejection of his message by the
unbelieving world.

c) This is why ONLY *eight* souls were saved
through water. Notice that they were
saved _____ water and
NOT _____ water.

i.   Again, notice that the eight who were
saved _____ got wet. It
was the disobedient persecutors and
rejectors of Noah's message that
died via the flood waters.

ii.   It would be odd then to use
_____ baptism as the

antitype, as Peter does in the next verse.

d) **Verse 21**: Type and antitype represent an
_____. The
TYPE here is the Ark saving people physically from the judgment of the flood waters and the *ANTITYPE* is baptism through the resurrection of Jesus Christ saving people spiritually.

e) The question becomes: what
_____ of baptism is Peter referencing here?

    i.   This baptism must represent God's
_____ (Jesus Christ = the Ark), saving the believer
_____ (from the wages of sin = the flood waters).

    ii.   God's spiritual salvation by placing each individual believer *IN* Jesus Christ (in union with Him through
_____ baptism. (See 1 Corinthians 12:13.) God's spiritual salvation is the *ANTITYPE* of God's physical salvation by placing Noah and his family in the Ark and

saving them from _____

judgment.

iii.   Ultimately, believers' salvation and position in righteousness before God is based upon their _____ with Jesus Christ. (See Romans 8:1 – "No condemnation to those who are _IN_ Christ Jesus." See 2 Corinthians 5:21 – "… that we might become the righteousness of God _IN_ Him.")

f)   This is _____ baptism, which is also described in Romans 6:3-4.

i.   Going under, represents our identification with Him in His death, which is also _____ in the Ark weathering the flood waters.

ii.   _Coming up_ represents our identification with Him in His resurrection, which is illustrated in the Ark landing on _____ _____ and starting life on a new earth.

APPENDIX 1

Types of Death in the Scripture

THE SEVEN DEATHS OF SCRIPTURE

	WHEN	CAUSE
1. SPIRITUAL	At conception	Born in Adam
2. PHYSICAL	When you die	The fall, curse, and being in Adam
3. ETERNAL	Begins when you physically die, lasts forever	Spiritual and physical death apart from faith in Christ
4. POSITIONAL	At the moment you get saved	Born again in Christ; Identification with Jesus Christ
5. TEMPORAL	During your Christian life, after salvation	Personal sin of the believer
6. OPERATIONAL	During your Christian life, after salvation	A failure to daily walk by faith resulting in a lack of Spirit- produced works
7. SEXUAL	During old age	Normal physical limitation

WHAT	VERSES	REMEDY
Separation of a person from God	Gen. 2:17 Eph. 2:1	Salvation: Being "Born Again"
Separation of your soul and spirit from your body	Heb. 9:27 Jn. 11:11-17	For a believer, it is only "sleep," then bodily resurrection
Separation of your body, soul, and spirit from God, forever	Rev. 20:14 Matt. 25:46	Salvation and receiving the gift of eternal life
Separation of the believer from all that he was in Adam	Rom. 6:3-6 Gal. 2:20	This is a remedy, as the believer is now dead to sin and alive unto God as a new creation in Christ
Separation from a right fellowship with God bringing His chastening	Luke 15:24 James 1:15 1 Tim. 5:6	Confession of sin and yielding to God
Separation from a right divine production, and a right testimony towards others	James 2:14-26 Heb. 6:1, 9:14	Confession of sin and dependence upon God & His grace provisions
Separation from the ability to physically reproduce	Rom. 4:17-19	Miracle from God

APPENDIX 2

160 Verses Proving Justification by Faith Alone

By: Dr. J. B. Hixson

There are approximately 160 verses in the NT that clearly state that salvation is solely based upon a person's faith, trust, or belief in Jesus Christ as savior.

Luke 7:48-50; 8:12; 18:42

John 1:7, 12; 2:23; 3:15, 16, 18, 36; 4:39; 4:41, 42; 5:24, 45-47; 6:29, 35, 40, 47; 7:38, 39; 8:24, 29, 30; 9:35-38; 10:24-26; 11:15, 25, 26, 41, 42; 12:36, 46; 13:19; 14:1-6, 17:20, 21; 19:35; 20:29, 31

Acts 3:16; 4:4, 32; 8:12, 37; 9:42; 10:43, 45; 11:17, 21; 13:21, 39; 14:1, 23, 27; 15:7, 9;16:31; 17:4, 5, 11, 12; 18:8, 27; 19:4; 20:21; 21:25; 26:18

Romans 1:16, 17; 3:22, 25, 26, 27, 28, 30; 4:3, 5, 9, 11, 13, 16, 23, 24; 5:1, 2; 9:30, 32,33; 10:4, 6, 9, 10; 11:20, 30-32; 15:13

1 Corinthians 1:21

2 Corinthians 4:4

Galatians 2:16, 20; 3:2, 5, 6, 7, 8, 9, 11, 14, 22, 24, 26; 5:5

Ephesians 1:13, 19; 2:8; 3:17

Philippians 1:29; 3:9

1 Thessalonians 1:7; 2:10; 4:14

2 Thessalonians 1:10; 2:12, 13; 3:2

1 Timothy 1:16; 3:16; 4:3, 10

2 Timothy 1:12; 3:15

Hebrews 4:2, 3; 6:12; 10:39; 11:6, 7, 31

James 2:23

1 Peter 1:21; 2:6, 7

1 John 5:1, 5, 10, 13

Jude 5

APPENDIX 3

Without the Shedding of Blood

"Without the shedding of blood there is no remission."
Hebrews 9:22

Activity[1]	Shedding of Blood?	Synonym for Faith?
Baptism	NO	NO
Commitment to God	NO	NO
Giving Money to the Poor	NO	NO
Meditation	NO	NO
Praying	NO	NO
Asking Jesus Into Your Heart	NO	NO
Confess Your Sins	NO	NO
Repent From Sins	NO	NO
Live Faithful to God	NO	NO
Death of Jesus Christ on the Cross	YES	YES

---

[1] Chart from Duluth Bible Church

APPENDIX 4

Different Versions of the Sinner's Prayer

The top three selling tracts of all time are *The Four Spiritual Laws* by Campus Crusade for Christ, *Steps to Peace With God* by the Billy Graham Evangelistic Association, and *This Was Your Life!* by Jack T. Chick. All three of these tracts contain a form of the sinner's prayer. Consider those and some others below.

1. *The Four Spiritual Laws by Bill Bright* verbalizes it this way: "Lord Jesus, I need You. Thank You for dying on the cross for my sins. I open the door of my life and receive You as my Savior and Lord. Thank You for forgiving my sins and giving me eternal life. Take control of the throne of my life. Make me the kind of person You want me to be."

2. *Steps to Peace With God by Billy Graham* verbalizes the prayer this way: "Dear Lord Jesus, I know that I am a sinner and need Your forgiveness. I believe that You died for my sins. I want to turn from my sins. I now invite You to come into my heart and life. I want to trust and follow You as Lord and Savior. In Jesus' name. Amen."

3. *This Was Your Life by Jack Chick* verbalizes the prayer this way: "Dear God, I am a sinner and need forgiveness. I

believe that Jesus Christ shed His precious blood and died for my sin. I am willing to turn from sin. I now invite Christ to come into my heart and life as my personal Saviour."

4. *3:16 The Numbers of Hope by Max Lucado* verbalizes the prayer this way: "Father, I believe you love me. You gave your one and only Son so I can live forever with you. Apart from you, I die. With you, I live. I choose life. I choose you."

5. *Steps to Assurance by Bible Study Fellowship* verbalizes the prayer this way: "O God, I know I have sinned. I have not obeyed your Word. I have tried to run my own life, ignoring you and your will for me. I have tried to decide for myself what is right and wrong. I know I deserve your wrath and punishment, and that I am lost unless you save me. I thank you for sending the Lord Jesus Christ to pay for my sin and guilt. I thank you for raising Him from the dead and giving Him authority over my life. I receive Him as my Savior and Lord. I receive your free gift of eternal life in Christ. I will turn from my sinful life to serve you, my Creator and Redeemer."

6. *Do You Know?* verbalizes the prayer this way: "Lord Jesus, thank You for Your gift of eternal life. I know I'm a sinner and do not deserve eternal life. But You loved me so You died and rose from the grave to purchase a place in heaven for me. I now trust in You alone for eternal

life and repent of my sin. Please take control as Lord of my life. Thank you so much!"

7. *The Only Way by Billy Graham* verbalizes the prayer this way: "O God, I am a sinner. I'm sorry for my sin. Forgive me. I want to turn from my sin. I receive Jesus Christ as my Savior; I confess Him as my Lord. From now on I want to follow Him. In Jesus' Name. Amen."

8. *The official Southern Baptist Convention website* verbalizes the prayer this way: "Lord Jesus, I know that I am a sinner and I do not deserve eternal life. But I believe You died and rose from the grave to make me a new creation and to prepare me to dwell in your presence forever. Jesus, come into my life, take control of my life, forgive my sins and save me. I am now placing my trust in You alone for my salvation and I accept your free gift of eternal life."

APPENDIX 5

Seven Baptisms of the Bible

Wet or dry?	Type of Baptism	Scripture
1a. Dry	1b. Baptism of Moses.	1c. 1 Corinthians 10:1-4.
2a. Dry	2b. Baptism of the Cup.	2c. Matthew 20:20-23; Luke 12:50.
3a. Dry	3b. Baptism by the Holy Spirit.	3c. Acts 1:4-5; Romans 6:3-4; 1 Corinthians 12:13; Ephesians 4:5; Galatians 3:26-28.
4a. Dry	4b. Baptism of Fire.	4c. Matthew 3:11-12; 13:24-30, 36-43, 49-50; Luke 3:16
5a. Wet	5b. Baptism of John.	5c. Matthew 3:1-11; John 1:25-33; Acts 19:1-4
6a. Wet	6b. Baptism of Jesus.	6c. Matthew 3:13-17
7a. Wet	7b. Baptism of Church-age Believers.	7c. Matthew 28:19-20; Acts 2:41, 8:26-40, 10:47-48, 18:8

Subject: Who is Baptized?	Sphere: Where are they baptized?	Results: Who or what identified with?
1d. Israelites.	1e. In the cloud and the sea.	1f. Identified with Moses.
2d. Christ.	2e. In suffering.	2f. Identified with the sins of the world.
3d. Church-age believers.	3e. In the body of Christ.	3f. Identified with Christ and other believers in His body.
4d. Unbelievers.	4e. In judgment fires of hell.	4f. Identified with God's judgment.
5d. John and Jesus' disciples (Israelites).	5e. In the Jordan river – Kingdom oriented.	5f. Publicly identified with the gospel of the kingdom and God's solution for righteousness.
6d. Jesus.	6e. In the Jordan river. – Will of the Father.	6f. Publicly identified with the repentant remnant AND confirmed the identity of Israel's Messiah.
7d. Church-age believers (disciples).	7e. In water – Discipleship oriented.	7f. Publicly identified with the gospel of grace AND union in Jesus Christ's body with other believers.

LESSON ONE ANSWERS

I. **IS**

   A.

      1. **gospel**

         a) **times**

      2. **special**

         a) **God's**

         b) **must**

   B.

      1. **saved**

      2. **need**

         a) **separated**

         b) **prove**

         c) **one**

      3. **consequence**

         a) **separation**

         b) **punish**

         c) **deserved**

         d) **never**

         e) **physical** - **spiritual** - **Second**

      4. **pay** - **perfect**

   C.

      1. **sinful**

         a) **ability**

         b) **believe**

      c) <u>anything</u>

  2. <u>only</u>

  3. <u>already</u>

  4. <u>process</u>

D.

  1. <u>must</u>

  2. <u>two</u>

      a) <u>person</u>

      b) <u>work</u>

  3.

      a) <u>Messiah</u>

      b) <u>human</u>

      c) <u>seed</u>

      d) <u>deity</u>

      e) <u>die</u> - <u>others</u>.

  4.

      a) <u>died</u>

         1) <u>Proof</u>

           (a) <u>scriptures</u>

           (b) <u>buried</u>

      b) <u>third</u>

         1) <u>Proof</u>

           (a) <u>scriptures</u>

           (b) <u>seen</u>

              (i) <u>Peter</u>

(ii) **twelve**

(iii) **500**

(iv) **half**

(v) **apostles**

(vi) **Paul**

5. **person** - **work**

E.

1. **required**

2. **faith**

   a) **160**

   b)

3.

   a) **rely upon**

   b) **object**

   c) **value** - **ability**

   d) **hearing**

   e) **works**

   f) **consistent**

   g) **work** - **gift**

LESSON TWO ANSWERS

II. <u>Not</u>

   A.

      1. <u>Two</u> - <u>debt</u> - <u>perfect</u>

      2. <u>Two</u> - <u>solution</u>.

      3. <u>already</u>

      4. <u>die</u> - <u>rise</u>

      5. <u>faith</u> - <u>solution</u>

   B.

      1. <u>contradictory</u>

      2. <u>examine</u>

      3. <u>disagree</u> - <u>clarity</u>

      4. <u>both</u>

         a. <u>grace</u>

         b. <u>yourselves</u>

         c. <u>clarity</u>

         d. <u>same</u> - <u>work</u>

         e. <u>ourselves</u>

      5. <u>facts</u>

      6. **<u>2,000</u>**

   C.

      1. <u>two</u>

      2. <u>multiple</u>

         a. <u>paid</u>

         b. <u>lamb</u>

      c. <u>completed</u>

      d. <u>one</u>

   3.

      a. <u>synonyms</u>

      b. <u>penalty</u>

      c. <u>spotlight</u>

      d. <u>additional</u>

D.

   1. <u>requirement</u>

   2. <u>same</u> - <u>not</u>.

   3.

      a. <u>remember</u>

         1) <u>day</u>

         2) <u>memory</u>

      b. <u>forgotten</u>

   4. <u>believe</u>

   5.

      a) <u>same</u>

         1) <u>agree</u>

         2) <u>emotions</u> - <u>synonym</u> - <u>sin</u>

      b.

         1) <u>Lord Jesus</u>

         2) <u>respect</u>

            a) <u>technical</u>

            b) <u>Yahweh</u>

c) <u>**version**</u>

d) <u>**same**</u>

c.

    1) <u>**saved**</u>

    2) <u>**context**</u>

        a) <u>**already**</u> - <u>**never**</u>

        b) <u>**himself**</u>

        c) <u>**already**</u>

        d) <u>**restore**</u> - <u>**become**</u>

        e) <u>**ask**</u> - <u>**wrong**</u>

E.

1. <u>**giving**</u>

2. <u>**bargained**</u>

3. <u>**backwards**</u>

LESSON THREE ANSWERS

A.

    1. <u>Two</u> - <u>debt</u> - <u>perfect</u>

    2. <u>Two</u> - <u>solution</u>.

    3. <u>already</u>

    4. <u>die</u> - <u>rise</u>

    5. <u>faith</u> - <u>solution</u>

B.

    1. <u>How</u> - <u>biblical</u>

    2. <u>synonymous</u>.

       a) <u>Doubt</u>

       b) <u>done</u>

          1)

          2)

          3)

          4)

       c) <u>already</u>

       d) <u>known</u> - <u>unknown</u>

       e) <u>unbelief</u>

    3. <u>one</u>

    4. <u>confess</u>

       a) <u>same</u>

       b) <u>asking</u>

    5. <u>includes</u> - <u>work</u>

    6. <u>anywhere</u>

a)

b)

    1) <u>already</u>

    2) <u>timeframe</u>

    3) <u>key</u>

        a) <u>covered</u> - <u>forgiven</u>

        b) <u>takes</u> <u>away</u>

        c) <u>New</u>

        d) <u>effects</u>

C.

  1. <u>Bible</u> - <u>example</u>

  2. <u>same</u>

  3. <u>repeating</u> - <u>already</u>

    a) <u>requirement</u>

    b) <u>narrative</u>

  4.

    a.

        1) <u>understanding</u>

           a) <u>one</u>

           b) <u>meticulous</u>

           c) <u>own</u>

           d) <u>additional</u> - <u>saved</u>

        2) <u>depending</u>

           a) <u>exhibiting</u>

           b) <u>save</u> - <u>already</u>

    b.

1) **prerequisite**

   a) **tribulation**

   b) **both**

2) **intended**

   a) **believed**

   b) **saved**

5. **moment**

LESSON FOUR ANSWERS

A.

1. <u>Two</u> - <u>debt</u> - <u>perfect</u>
2. <u>Two</u> - <u>solution</u>
3. <u>already</u>
4. <u>die</u> - <u>rise</u>
5. <u>faith</u> - <u>solution</u>

B.

1. <u>verbal</u>
   a) <u>wrong</u>
   b) <u>enough</u> - <u>complete</u>
2. <u>mute</u> - <u>publicly</u>
3. <u>biblical</u>
   a) <u>earns</u>
   b) <u>saved</u>
4. <u>official</u> - <u>moment</u>
5.
   a.
   1) <u>lynchpin</u>
   2) <u>formula</u>
   3) <u>changes</u>
      a) <u>obstacles</u>
      b) <u>near</u> - <u>available</u>
      c) <u>modifications</u>
      d) <u>do</u> - <u>believe</u>

4)

    a) <u>same</u>

        i.   <u>sin</u>

        ii.   <u>title</u>

        iii.   **Yahweh**

        iv.   **God** - **agree**

        v.   **True** - **believed**

        vi.   **opposite**

    b)

        i.   **delineate**

        ii.   <u>rose</u> - <u>accepted</u>

    c) <u>domino</u>

5) <u>order</u> - <u>follows</u>

6) <u>distinct</u>

    a) <u>penalty</u>

        i.   <u>obtains</u>

        ii.   <u>believes</u>

    b) **tribulation**

        i.   <u>synonymous</u>

        ii.   **Tribulation**

        iii.   <u>preceded</u>

        iv.   <u>faith</u>

        v.   <u>born</u> <u>again</u>

        vi.   <u>generation</u> - <u>already</u>

Extra Study

b.

    1) <u>conditional</u>

    2) <u>assume</u>

    3) <u>assume</u>

       a) <u>with</u>

       b) <u>guarantee</u> - <u>promise</u>

    4) <u>assume</u>

       a) <u>under</u>

       b) <u>perfectly</u>

       c) <u>administration</u>

       d) <u>endure</u> - <u>solely</u>

    5) <u>assume</u>

       a) <u>loss</u> - <u>denying</u>

       b) <u>reward</u>

       c) <u>publicly</u> - <u>potential</u>

    6)

       a) <u>bold</u>

       b) <u>presently</u>

       c) <u>Himself</u>

          i. <u>promises</u>

          ii. <u>work</u> - <u>value</u>

          iii. <u>character</u>

          iv. <u>union</u>

LESSON FIVE ANSWERS

A.

    1. <u>Two</u> - <u>debt</u> - <u>perfect</u>

    2. <u>Two</u> - <u>solution</u>

    3. <u>already</u>

    4. <u>die</u> - <u>rise</u>

    5. <u>faith</u> - <u>solution</u>

B.

    1. <u>popular</u>

       a) <u>**5,000**</u>

    2. <u>never</u>

       a. <u>never</u>

          1) <u>saved</u>

          2) <u>read</u>

       b. <u>saved</u>

          1) <u>faith</u>

             a) <u>doubt</u>

             b) <u>already</u>

             c) <u>known</u> - <u>unknown</u>

             d) <u>unbelief</u>

             e) <u>ask</u> - <u>result</u>

       c. <u>understanding</u>

          1) <u>knowing</u>

          2) <u>Christ</u>

             a) <u>necessary</u>

        b) **misplaced** - **finished**

   3) **good news** - **wrong**

d. **assurance** - **false**

   1) **saved**

      a) **once**

      b) **focus**

      c) **object** - **event**

      d) **unreliable**

   2) **alone**

   3) **uncertainty**

      a) **come in**

      b) **sincere**

      c) **right**

      d) **know**

   4) **doing** - **already**

e. **teach**

   1) **found**

   2) **church**

   3) **unbeliever**

      a) **correcting** - **rebuking**

      b) **success** - **different**

   4) **church**

      a) **church** - **inside**

      b) **fellowship**

LESSON SIX ANSWERS

A.

1. <u>Two</u> - <u>debt</u> - <u>perfect</u>

2. <u>Two</u> – <u>solution</u>

3. <u>already</u>

4. <u>die</u> - <u>rise</u>

5. <u>faith</u> - <u>solution</u>

B.

1. <u>Of</u> - <u>from</u>

2. <u>Demand</u>

3.

   a) <u>Change</u> - <u>mind</u>

   b) <u>Mind</u>

   c) <u>Faulty</u>

   d) <u>Original</u> - <u>context</u>

   e) <u>Gay</u> - <u>homosexual</u>

4.

   a.

   1) <u>Mind</u>

   2) <u>Kill</u> - <u>participants</u>

   b.

   1) <u>plans</u>

   2) <u>minds</u> - <u>again</u>

   c.

   1) <u>twenty</u>

      a) **God**

      b) **Proverbs**

      c) minds

5. sin - **good**.

6. who - what

    a) believe

    b) blank

7. **wrong**

    a) history

    b) prior to

      1) death

      2) reacted

    c) post - feeling - confessing - penance

    d) **Latin**

    e) retained

      1) penitence

      2) standard

      3) relied

      4) same - carryover

8. turn

    a. less than

      1) mystery

      2) habitually

      3) habitual

        a) **Biblical**

        b) never - truly

      4) <u>new</u> - <u>lost</u>

  b. <u>less</u> - <u>works-oriented</u>

  c. <u>conduct</u> – <u>thinking</u>

  d. <u>contradicts</u> - <u>need</u> - <u>help</u>

  e. <u>past</u> - <u>full</u>

Extra Study

9. <u>context</u>

  a. <u>audience</u>

    1) <u>righteousness</u>

    2) <u>meant</u> - <u>trusting</u>

  b. <u>audience</u>

    1) <u>identity</u>

    2) <u>worthy</u>

  c. <u>audience</u>

    1) <u>approach</u>

    2) <u>minds</u>

    3) <u>believe</u> - <u>way</u>

  d. <u>audience</u>

    1) <u>two</u> - <u>Who</u>

    2) <u>polytheism</u>

  e. <u>audience</u>

    1)

    2) <u>repent</u> - <u>turning</u> - <u>works</u>

      a) <u>distinct</u> - <u>synonymous</u>

      b) <u>distinct</u> – <u>behavior</u>

LESSON SEVEN ANSWERS

A.
1. <u>Two</u> - <u>debt</u> - <u>perfect</u>
2. <u>Two</u> – <u>solution</u>
3. <u>already</u>
4. <u>die</u> - <u>rise</u>
5. <u>faith</u> - <u>solution</u>

B.
1. <u>confuses</u>
   a) <u>submit</u>
   b) <u>saved</u>
      1) <u>only</u>
      2) <u>additional</u>
2. <u>accurate</u>
   a. <u>confess</u>
      1) <u>same</u>
      2) <u>respect</u>
      3) <u>technical</u> - <u>Yahweh</u>
      4) <u>unbelieving</u> - <u>agree</u>
   b. <u>sanctification</u>
      1) <u>confuses</u>
      2) <u>never</u> - <u>twice</u> - <u>once</u>
         a) <u>requirement</u>
         b) <u>justification</u>

         3) <u>obedient</u> - <u>justify</u>

   c. <u>assurance</u>.

         1) <u>know</u> - <u>moment</u>

         2) <u>denied</u>

         3) <u>no one</u>

         4) <u>faithfully</u> - <u>never</u> - <u>finished</u>

   d. <u>carnal</u>

         1) <u>promote</u>

         2) <u>fully</u>

            a) <u>never</u>

            b) <u>driving</u>

         3) <u>are</u>

            a) <u>genuine</u>

               i. <u>believers</u>

               ii. <u>every</u>

            b) <u>ongoing</u>

               i. <u>ongoing</u> - <u>possible</u>

            c) <u>present</u> - <u>continual</u>

   e. <u>*should*</u> - <u>*must*</u>

         1) <u>habitually</u>

         2) <u>cannot</u>

         3) <u>presence</u>

            a) <u>ability</u>

            b) <u>potential</u>

         4) <u>subjunctive</u>

            a) <u>probable</u> - <u>possibility</u>

b) **factual**

c) *should* - *must*

    i.

        a) **desires** - **guaranteed**.

    ii.

        a) **desires** - **guaranteed**

    iii.

        a) **desires** - **guaranteed**

    iv.

        a) **desires** - **guaranteed**

LESSON EIGHT ANSWERS

A.

1. <u>Two</u> - <u>debt</u> - <u>perfect</u>
2. <u>Two</u> – <u>solution</u>
3. <u>already</u>
4. <u>die</u> - <u>rise</u>
5. <u>faith</u> - <u>solution</u>

B.

1. <u>testimony</u>
2. <u>identify</u>
   a) <u>Greek</u>
   b) <u>water</u>
3.
   a. <u>wet</u> - <u>four</u>
   b. <u>context</u>
   c. <u>alone</u>
      1) <u>seven</u>
      2) <u>proof</u> - <u>fit</u> - <u>fit</u>
   d. <u>emphasis</u>
   e. <u>message</u>
   f. <u>essential</u> - <u>action</u> - <u>behavior</u>
   g. <u>for</u> - <u>completed</u>
4.
   a) <u>Regulated</u> - <u>sin</u>

b) <u>probation</u> - <u>character</u>

c) <u>immersion</u> - <u>three</u>

d) <u>leader</u> - <u>receive</u>

e) <u>original</u> - <u>original</u>

f) <u>only</u>

5. <u>means</u>

a. <u>command</u> - <u>how</u>

1) <u>only</u>

2) <u>modifying</u>

3)

    a) <u>intentional</u>

    b) <u>wisdom</u>

4)

    a) <u>identification</u>

    b) <u>visual</u>

    c) <u>partners</u>

Extra Study

6.

a.

1) <u>seven</u> - <u>common</u>

2) <u>Spirit</u> - <u>common</u> - <u>automatically</u>

3)

    a) <u>two</u>

    b) <u>two</u>

    c) <u>connection</u>

        d) <u>unites</u>

b.

  1) <u>context</u>

    a) <u>repeated</u>

    b) <u>Great</u>

    c) <u>difference</u>

    d) <u>disciple</u> - <u>how</u>

  2) <u>teaching</u>

    a) <u>somebody else</u> - <u>available</u>

    b) <u>alone</u> - <u>more than</u>

    c) <u>text</u> - <u>saved</u>

    d) <u>text</u> - <u>condemned</u>

      i. <u>sit down</u>

      ii. <u>bus</u> - <u>sitting down</u>

      iii. <u>discipleship</u> - <u>requirement</u>

    e) <u>saved</u> - *NOT*

      i. <u>dropped</u>

c.

  1) <u>context</u>

    a) <u>use</u> - <u>alone</u>

      i. <u>regeneration</u> - <u>alone</u>

      ii. <u>once</u>

    b) <u>illustrations</u>

      i. <u>tutor</u>

      ii. <u>adoption</u>

      iii. <u>toga</u>

      2)
- a) <u>spiritual</u>
  - i. <u>death</u> – <u>Moses</u> - <u>Body</u>
  - ii. <u>dry</u> - <u>people</u>
- b) <u>know</u>
- c) <u>man</u> - <u>God</u>
- d) <u>baptized</u>

d.

    1) <u>context</u>
- a) <u>necessity</u>
- b) <u>confuse</u>
- c) <u>surprised</u>
  - i. <u>explanation</u>
  - ii. <u>explain</u> - <u>Old</u>

    2)
- a) <u>indirect</u> - <u>rabbi</u>
- b) <u>glance</u>
  - i. <u>both</u> - <u>same</u>
  - ii. <u>renewal</u>
  - iii. <u>new</u>
  - iv. <u>water</u>
  - v. <u>Spirit</u>
  - vi. <u>enter</u>
- c) <u>miraculous</u>
- d) <u>bones</u> - <u>wind</u>

e.

1) <u>context</u>

   a) <u>descended</u>

   b) <u>validate</u>

   c) <u>languages</u>

   d) <u>drunk</u> - <u>later</u>

      i. <u>outpouring</u>

   e) <u>sermon</u>

   f) <u>responsibility</u>

   g) <u>mistake</u> - <u>judgment</u>

      i. <u>languages</u>

2) <u>observations</u>

   a) <u>history</u>

   b) <u>repentance</u>

      i. <u>Great</u>

      ii. <u>repentance</u> - <u>Repent</u> - <u>repentance</u>

      iii. <u>precedes</u> - <u>involvement</u>

   c) <u>absent</u> - <u>Baptism</u>

   d) <u>only</u>

      i. <u>only</u>

      ii. <u>only</u>

      iii. <u>only</u>

      iv. <u>alone</u>

3) <u>context</u>

   a) <u>do</u>

      i. <u>Believe</u>

   b) <u>broad</u> - <u>few</u>

      i. <u>full</u> - <u>disciples</u>

      ii. <u>comprehensive</u> - <u>Disciple</u>

  c) <u>plural</u>

  d) <u>singular</u>

  e) <u>All</u> - <u>he</u>

  f) <u>preposition</u>

      i. *<u>resting</u>*

      ii. <u>resting</u>

      iii. <u>resting</u>

4) <u>change</u> - <u>discipleship</u>

f.

  1) <u>context</u>

    a) <u>conversion</u>

    b) <u>against</u>

    c) <u>crazy</u>- <u>forbidden</u>

    d) <u>address</u>

    e) <u>only</u>

  2) <u>teaching</u>

    a) <u>before</u> - <u>after</u>

      i. <u>other</u>

      ii. <u>already</u> - <u>appointed</u>

      iii. <u>Brother</u>

      iv. <u>before</u>

    b) <u>extending</u>

      i. <u>shock</u> - <u>frozen</u>

    c) <u>commands</u>

d) **participles**

  i. **connected** - **connected**

  ii. **first**

  iii. **first**

e) **already**

  i.   **appealed** - **believers**

  ii.   **believe**

  iii. **one**

  iv.   **affected** - **God** - **agent**

  v.   **fellowship**

  vi.   **conscience**

f) **Great**

  i. **publicly**

g.

1) **context**

  a) **persecution**

  b) **suffering**

  c) **unjustly**

  d) **patience**

  e) **believing**

  f) **respond**

  g) **trust**

2) **additional**

  a) **wicked**

  b) **specific**

  c) **root**

           i. **Ark**

          ii. **preparation** - **rejection**

          iii. **exhibited**

  d) **shut**

  e) **in** – **Ark** - **water**

3) **full**

  a) **preached**

      i. **unbelievers**

     ii. **through**

  b) **patient**

  c) **through** - **by**

      i. **never**

     ii. **water**

  d) **illustration**

  e) **kind**

      i. **provision** - **spiritually**

     ii. **Spirit** - **physical**

     iii. **union**

  f) **spiritual**

      i. **illustrated**

     ii. **dry land**

RECOMMENDED RESOURCES

Gospel Response Cliché #1: Believe and Confess Your Sins

Gospel Response Cliché #2: Give Your Heart or Life to God

Gospel Response Cliché #3: Ask for Forgiveness

Gospel Response Cliché #4: Pray the Sinner's Prayer

Gospel Response Cliché #5: You Must Make a Public Profession of Faith

1. Stegall, Thomas L. *Salvation in Romans 10:9-13*. Duluth, MN: Grace Gospel Press, 2021. (Free Download: https://www.gracegospelpress.org/free-downloads/)

Gospel Response Cliché #6: Ask Jesus Into Your Heart

1. Rokser, Dennis M. *Seven Reasons Not to Ask Jesus Into Your Heart*. Duluth, MN: Grace Gospel Press, 2007. (Free Download: https://www.gracegospelpress.org/free-downloads/)

Gospel Response Cliché #7: Repent "from" OR Repent "of" Your Sins

1. Cocoris, G. Michael. *Repentance: The Most Misunderstood Word in the Bible*. Milwaukee, WI: Grace Gospel Press, 2010. (Free Download: http://www.disciplesbibleinstitute.com/repentance.html)

2. Seymour, Richard A. *All About Repentance*. LaGrange, WY: Integrity Press, 2007.

Gospel Response Cliché #8: Make Christ Lord of Your Life –
Lordship Salvation

1. Bing, Charles C. *Lordship Salvation: A Biblical Evaluation and Response*. Burleson, TX: Grace Life Ministries, 1991.

2. Bing, Charles C. "Some Questions for the Lordship Salvationist." *Grace Family Journal 4 (*March-April 2001): 10.

3. Clark, John. *A Faulty Foundation*: *How Lordship Salvation Negatively Impacts the Christian Life*. Newnan, GA: Tetelestai Press, 2021. (Free Download: https://www.gracenewnan.org/biblicalresources)

4. Rokser, Dennis M. "Examining Lordship Salvation Pt. 1: Weighed in the Balances and Found Wanting." *Grace Family Journal 10* (Summer 2007): 4-8. (Free Download: https://www.gracegospelpress.org/grace-family-journal-editions/)

5. Rokser, Dennis M. "Examining Lordship Salvation: Weighed in the Balances and Found Wanting Pt. 2." *Grace Family Journal 10* (Fall 2007): 10-18. (Free Download: https://www.gracegospelpress.org/grace-family-journal-editions/)

6. Rokser, Dennis M. "Examining Lordship Salvation Pt. 3: Weighed in the Balances and Found Wanting." *Grace Family Journal 11* (Spring 2008): 9-14. (Free Download: https://www.gracegospelpress.org/grace-family-journal-editions/)

7. Rokser, Dennis M. "Examining Lordship Salvation Pt. 4." *Grace Family Journal 11* (Summer 2008): 23-27. (Free Download: https://www.gracegospelpress.org/grace-family-journal-editions/)

8. Rokser, Dennis M. "Examining Lordship Salvation Pt. 5." *Grace Family Journal 11* (Fall 2008): 11-15. (Free Download: https://www.gracegospelpress.org/grace-family-journal-editions/)

9. Rokser, Dennis M. "Examining Lordship Salvation Pt. 6." *Grace Family Journal 11* (Winter 2008): 2-11. (Free Download: https://www.gracegospelpress.org/grace-family-journal-editions/)

10. Rokser, Dennis M. "Examining Lordship Salvation Pt. 7." *Grace Family Journal 12* (Spring 2009): 2-5. (Free Download: https://www.gracegospelpress.org/grace-family-journal-editions/)

11. Rokser, Dennis M. "Examining Lordship Salvation Pt. 8." *Grace Family Journal 12* (Summer 2009): 2-5. (Free Download: https://www.gracegospelpress.org/grace-family-journal-editions/)

12. Rokser, Dennis M. "Examining Lordship Salvation Pt. 9." *Grace Family Journal 12* (Fall 2009): 2-4. (Free Download: https://www.gracegospelpress.org/grace-family-journal-editions/)

13. Rokser, Dennis M. "Examining Lordship Salvation Pt. 10." *Grace Family Journal 12* (Winter 2009): 2-4. (Free

Download: https://www.gracegospelpress.org/grace-family-journal-editions/)

Gospel Response Cliché #9: Believe and Be Baptized in Water – Baptismal Regeneration

1. Corcoris, G. Michael. "Is Water Baptism Necessary for Salvation?" *Chafer Theological Seminary Journal* vol. 3, no. 1 (Summer 1997). (Free Download: http://www.disciplesbibleinstitute.com/is-baptism-necessary-for-salvation.html)

2. Merryman, Ron. "Acts 2:38: An Exposition – Must One be Water Baptized to be Saved?" *Grace Family Journal 1* (July-August 1998): 13-15. (Free Download: https://www.gracegospelpress.org/grace-family-journal-editions/)

3. Rokser, Dennis M. *Seven Key Questions About Water Baptism*. Duluth, MN: Grace Gospel Press, 2007. (Free Download: https://www.gracegospelpress.org/free-downloads/)

4. Stegall, Tom. "Another Look at Acts 2:38 & the Gospel, Pt. 1." *Grace Family Journal 12* (Spring 2009): 12-19. (Free Download: https://www.gracegospelpress.org/grace-family-journal-editions/)

5. Stegall, Tom. "Another Look at Acts 2:38 & the Gospel, Pt. 2." *Grace Family Journal 12* (Summer 2009): 9-16. (Free Download: https://www.gracegospelpress.org/grace-family-journal-editions/)

6. Zeller, George. "Does Water Baptism Save? A Biblical Refutation of Baptismal Regeneration." *Middletown Bible Church.* Accessed December 31, 2023. https://www.middletownbiblechurch.org/salvatio/baptsave.htm.

For more FREE biblical resources, go to www.gracenewnan.org and select the "Biblical Resources" tab.

For more teaching from Pastor John Clark, please visit www.gracenewnan.org.

SCRIPTURE INDEX

OLD TESTAMENT

NEW TESTAMENT

Romans

ABOUT THE AUTHOR

Dr. John Thomas Clark holds his bachelor's degree in Mathematics from the University of Texas at San Antonio, has a master's degree in Theology (Th.M.) from Tyndale Theological Seminary and Biblical Institute, and his doctorate degree (DMin) with an emphasis on expository preaching from Dallas Theological Seminary. He values systematic, verse-by-verse Bible teaching and enjoys drawing out truths from the original languages. John has served as the Senior Pastor of Grace Community Fellowship in Newnan, Georgia since September 2016.

Additionally, John was a founding board member of DM2 (Disciple Makers Multiplied), a mission organization focused on pastoral training and discipleship of other disciple-makers. John still leads DM2's field to Liberia, Africa and travels there twice a year to train pastors.

John's first and foremost ministry lies in being a husband to his wife, Carrie, and a loving father to their five children. For more teaching from Pastor John Clark, please visit www.gracenewnan.org.

.

www.ingramcontent.com/pod-product-compliance
Lightning Source LLC
LaVergne TN
LVHW051731080426

835511LV00018B/2993

9 781735 335971